Saturday Meditations from the
𝕿𝖍𝖊 𝕯𝖆𝖎𝖑𝖞 𝕿𝖊𝖑𝖊𝖌𝖗𝖆𝖕𝖍

Rainbows through the Rain

by

Denis Duncan

The sequel to *Be Still and Know...*, and
Solitude, Stillness and Serenity

DEDICATION

I dedicate this third book of Meditations – as I did the first (*Be Still and Know...*) and the second (*Solitude, Stillness, Serenity*) – to my wife Ettie, who died on 16th October 1993 and who was for 51 years my partner on the way.

As she served on the staff of the *Daily Telegraph* for over twenty years, particularly as secretary to Max Hastings, then Editor-in-Chief, it is even more appropriate that these volumes of Saturday Meditations from that paper should be dedicated to her.

ALSO BY DENIS DUNCAN:

Be Still and Know ...
Solitude, Stillness, Serenity
A Day at a Time
Creative Silence
Health and Healing: A Ministry to Wholeness
Love, the Word that Heals
Here is My Hand

BOOKS EDITED BY DENIS DUNCAN

Through the Year with William Barclay • *Every Day with William Barclay* • *Marching Orders* • *Marching On* • *Through the Year with J. B. Phillips* • *Through the Year with Cardinal Heenan*

Denis Duncan is a minister of the Church of Scotland, a former editor of *British Weekly* and Director of the Churches' Council for Health and Healing. He was also Associate Director and Training Supervisor at Westminster Pastoral Foundation, Director of Highgate Counselling Centre, and of Hampstead Counselling Service, all in London. Earlier he served in St. Margaret's Parish in Juniper Green, Edinburgh, and in Trinity/Duke Street Parish, Glasgow. The focus of his current ministry is 'proclamation through preaching, writing and the ministry of healing'.

Copyright © 2000 John Hunt Publishing Ltd
Text © 2000 Denis Duncan in conjunction with the *Daily Telegraph*

ISBN 1 903019 70 2

Typography: Graham Whiteman

Write to:
John Hunt Publishing Ltd
46A West Street
Alresford
Hampshire SO24 9AU
UK

The rights of Denis Duncan as author of this work have been asserted in accordance with the Copyright, Designs and Patents Act 1988.

A CIP catalogue record for this book is available from the British Library.

Printed in Guernsey, Channel Islands

Contents

Introduction

The publication of the third book of Meditations that I have contributed week by week to the Saturday edition of the *Daily Telegraph* marks the completion of ten years of this ministry through print. In all, I have provided over 250 such contributions: 100 as *Be Still and Know . . .* in 1994 and a further 75 followed in 1997 under the title *Solitude, Stillness and Serenity. Rainbows Through the Rain* brings together the subsequent 75 contributions.

I find a particular sense of privilege in writing devotional material for the largest national 'heavy', the *Daily Telegraph*. With a circulation of well over one million copies, and an estimated readership of over three million people, an opportunity for ministry on a huge scale is provided. If only a small proportion of that readership reads the Meditations, it is a congregation far in excess of that encountered in years of preaching. I am fortunate indeed to have been given this opportunity.

In writing for a wide range of readers, from the academic to the man or woman in the street or pew, my essential purpose is pastoral. My many years of involvement in the parish ministry, specialist pastoral ministry and healing ministry have made me aware of the depth and extent of human suffering, bereavement, anxiety and emotional pain. I try therefore to bring comfort and encouragement, biblically based, to all, stressing the reality of forgiveness and the possibility of new life. I point too to the wonders of God's creation, the mystery of salvation and the ministry of reconciliation as positive features of faith.

I express my continuing gratitude to Charles Moore, Editor of the *Daily Telegraph*, for allowing me to effect this ministry and, being supportive of it; to the leader page secretaries and features sub-editors who see the copy through each week, and to Jillian Tallon who has produced the copy for each of my 250 Meditations. I also acknowledge the sympathetic co-operation of John Hunt, Managing Director of John Hunt Publishing.

Rainbows through the Rain

A memorable image, one that is worthy of being carried over into a new century, is that of the rainbow over the Rheinfall in Switzerland. It was on an October day that my friend Jillian and I sailed across the Rhine in a small boat to take a closer look at the turbulent waterfall at Schaffhausen. For thousands of years the cascade has thundered down to create stormy waters and swirling torrents, but when the sun shines brightly – as it did that day – it projects a striking rainbow through the vast spray thrown up by the waterfall. It seemed so close, possibly 30 m (100 ft) above the water, colourful and complete. That rainbow, shining through the turbulence, is not only a wonderful sight, but a dramatic symbol.

The rainbow above the churning waters is an appropriate image for a new year, a new century, a new millennium, for just such a symbol for the new world was offered after the great flood, in the Old Testament story. 'I will set my rainbow in the clouds,' God said to Noah, 'and it will be the sign of the covenant between me and the earth. Whenever the rainbow appears in the clouds, I will see it and remember the everlasting covenant'. The rainbow proclaimed God's continuing presence despite the clouds and storms.

Jesus, we are told, came to be 'God with us'. The Incarnation was no mere form of words. It was pulsating action, expressing love and compassion. These qualities, divine in their nature, became incarnate in living encounters with people. That Jesus suffered as human beings do, was tempted as we are, and shared our lot, is made known in his miracles of healing, his empathy in bereavement, his understanding and forgiveness of human failure. Sharing and caring was fundamental to his mission, whether he talked tenderly but firmly to a woman caught in an act of adultery, loved a reluctant, rich young ruler, conversed patiently but authoritatively with a respected senior citizen such as

Nicodemus, or ministered to a woman from Samaria. In every human situation where there is panic, pain or peril we are not alone; 'God with us' indeed.

The new century will increase efforts to find contemporary language and meaningful metaphors that will make the credal truths, on which faith is based, relevant to the people of the new millennium. It is however the language and the images that need to change, not the faith, 'the things in which we most surely believe'. They, like the One to whom they relate, are 'the same – yesterday, today and for ever'.

At the heart of belief is the divine–human relationship, proclaimed in the Old Testament and confirmed by Jesus, a relationship expressed in the eternal triangle of love between God, ourselves and our neighbour. It exists because 'He first loved us'. The rainbow in the rain is the symbol of the promised presence of 'God with us' whatever our situation. Look carefully and you will trace rainbows through the rain.

01. The Spiritual Pilgrimage

Beauty and Holiness

Every act of worship should magnify beauty and holiness. Whether two or three gather together or a multitude assembles for praise and prayer, the Psalmist's exhortation is to 'Worship the Lord in the beauty of holiness'. He would surely accept too, the holiness of beauty. No one should leave an act of worship without experiencing the wonder that leads to awe, reverence and rededication, a new realization of the presence of the risen Christ, and gratitude for the comfort that comes from the God who is with us. The privilege of worship is, for those who come to it, the opportunity to touch and handle things unseen, but it is also a mighty responsibility for those who are asked to lead it – those who, with true humility, extend the great invitation: 'Let us worship God'.

The created world is a very beautiful place. To watch the extraordinary sunrises and sunsets in Scotland this winter can only result in a grand 'Amen'. The flowers that bloom so brilliantly in the spring, birds on the wing, animals running wild . . . we all have our own evidence of the wonder of creation. And in the world of the arts, magnificent writing, striking sculpture, 'poet's pen and painter's hand' lift the human spirit above the mundane and the ordinary. The genius of Mozart, a Beethoven symphony, a Bach motet, a Schubert sonata, can all provide inspiration that touches the deep places of the soul. Why is it then that the world has to be cursed by the tawdriness and triviality of so much modern activity? That the lives and loves of so-called celebrities are made more important than the suffering of Kosovo? That the sacred intimacies of relationships and the grief of bereavement become the butt of comedians' humour? That a conscious desire to push boundaries back as far as possible typifies many approaches to entertainment? There is an ominous phrase in the Book of Judges – 'every man did that which was right in his own eyes'. In a society where religion and politics were intertwined, such crass individualism could only lead to anarchy. There are many today who claim that we too have the right to do whatever we like. But that will bring moral and spiritual anarchy.

Unless there is some objective standard against which to test our intentions, motives, behaviour and policies, the danger of moral, ethical and spiritual anarchy is real. It is through religion that, for most people, that standard is provided. For Christians, the very core of Jesus's teaching demands that because human beings are made in the image of God, they must never be used as a means to an end. Any behaviour or policy that demeans or damages someone else must always be questioned. It is responsible community, not rampant individualism, that is at the heart of the gospel.

Keep ugliness at bay or beauty and holiness will be its victims.

True Serenity

The most effective contribution to the communication of the gospel is the genuinely holy life. If this principle was ever in doubt, it has been hugely reaffirmed through the ministry, in life and in death, of Cardinal Basil Hume. Across the denominations, from members of other faiths and those with none, from prominent people in high places to humble souls in every walk of life, has come the recognition of a spirituality that was indeed profound. Such goodness brings a response that has nothing to do with shared dogma or credal conformity. It is an instinctive reaction to demonstrated holiness.

Paul, writing to Timothy, was greatly concerned to ensure that, living in 'crooked and depraved times', his commitment to spiritual fundamentals was essential. To hold on to sound teaching when false prophets seek to destroy the faith becomes a priority. 'Guard the good deposit that was entrusted to you,' he writes to Timothy, 'guard it with the help of the Holy Spirit who lives in us'. But it is not only a holding action that is needed. Spirituality must develop new depths. To ensure that growth, a further step is involved: 'Fan into flame the gift of God,' he says.

To live what Paul calls 'the holy life' within the security of the monastery is one thing, but to have to do it when walking the corridors of ecclesiastical power, surrounded by (and subject to) political pressures, is a wholly different matter. It was the capacity to hold to the life of devotion and retreat despite the conflicts of present-day public life that Basil Hume demonstrated. His epitaph will proclaim his simplicity, his sincerity and his serenity in a world of confusion, intrigue and turmoil.

Of those gifts of simplicity, sincerity and serenity, it is the last that has so moved people everywhere. In a position of power in politics and public affairs, he was ever available to the man, woman or child in the street. That has touched the hearts of many. Insincerity in high places has brought huge international problems and colossal human suffering in Ireland, the Balkans and the Middle East. In a position where he had controversial issues to face, he could make mistakes yet never lose his sincerity. That was an enormous influence for good. But his final public testimony to his coming death evidenced a serenity that gave wings to his own words in his book, *The Mystery of the Cross* [2]: 'Death is a formidable foe until we learn to make it a friend. Death is to be feared if we do not learn to welcome it. Death is the ultimate absurdity if we do not see it as fulfilment. Death haunts us when viewed as a journey into nothingness rather than a pilgrimage to a place where true happiness is found . . . Death is not the end of the road, but a gateway to a better place'. To attain to such authentic serenity is a triumph of grace indeed.

2. *The Mystery of the Cross,* by Basil Hume, Darton Longman & Todd, 1998.

Through Pain to Peace

There is something very dramatic about a statement in the story of doubting Thomas, the disciple whose belief in the resurrection of Jesus had to be 'evidence-based'. In John's Gospel we read 'And Jesus came, the doors being shut.' In literal terms, it is simply the record of a fact. The risen Lord did appear in their midst although the doors were closed. What is moving about the phrase is the symbolic truth encapsulated in it. It is another way of saying that 'Man's extremity is God's opportunity'. It is in the depths of our despair, when we do not know where to go or what to do, when all the doors to progress seem shut, that Jesus comes in grace to be 'God with us'.

It is that very point which is expressed with great power by St. Paul in his second letter to the Corinthians, a letter that keeps hopelessness and hope in close relationship. 'We are under pressure on every side,' he writes (in William Barclay's translation), 'but never without a way out. We are at our wits' end, but never at our hope's end. We are pursued by men but never abandoned by God. We are knocked down but never knocked out.' It is, Paul tells the Corinthian Christians, when they are at their lowest ebb that they will find that 'the supreme power belongs to God and does not have its source in us'.

It would be easy to dismiss such language as pious talk or religious sentimentality were it not the case that so many would willingly testify to such an experience. People with physical disabilities, emotional agony or even spiritual torment, have found that meeting the pressures and the knock-out blows with faith allows them to discover that precisely at the point of crisis, there are the seeds of victory. A seriously disabled woman, incapacitated from birth and later totally blind, is somehow able to say that 'the best things I have done for God have been done since – and because – I

12

became blind'. A victim of acute suffering and appalling pain can manage a radiant smile as she talks of the privilege of 'sharing in the sufferings of my Lord'. So often the journey of discipleship has its source in the depths, the experience (in the words of the Psalmist) of emerging from 'the miry clay' to find one's feet 'on the rock'. The Psalmist also declares that it is when people are 'at their wits' end that they cry unto the Lord'.

The journey to inner peace may well be through the experience of pain. It does not however need to be so. If we return to the story of Thomas, we will remember the encouragement conveyed by Jesus's words to Thomas. The disciple was blessed, in that he could base his faith on experience, but greatly blessed too, said Jesus, are those who believe without such evidence. It is possible to learn the glorious truth about the 'supreme power of God' without having to journey through despair and pain. Fortunate are those who have come to such a faith.

God's Generosity

'It is in the silence of the desert that the battle for the life or death of the soul will be decided, for there the false, the trivial, the decorative is stripped away and human beings come face to face with themselves and with God.' I wrote these words in 1980 [3], and they remain true in terms of subsequent experience. It is indeed in the silence that we come to terms with ourselves and with God. I had not then, however, come across a statement seeming to confirm this analysis of the spiritual life, in the writings of the great reformer, John Calvin. He wrote: 'Nearly all the wisdom we possess, that is to say true and sound wisdom, consists of two parts. These are "knowledge of God and of ourselves".' He continues: 'Although they are closely connected, it is difficult to say which comes first. Knowledge of ourselves not only stimulates us to seek God but, as it were, also leads us by the hand to find him . . . We never achieve a clear knowledge of ourselves unless we have first looked upon God's face and then descended from contemplating him to examining ourselves.'

The desert place experience (and 'desert' means wherever that personal, private sanctuary is) ought to be profound. It may well create a sense of apprehension because the process is a threatening one but it should be healing. No process of self-examination in the light of God's presence can be other than painful. Laid out behind us is the seemingly endless sequence of personal failures, innocent errors, wilful disobediences, the repetition of surrendered sins, the sense of incomprehension at the depths to which publicly personable people can sink. But it is precisely here that the time – or rather timeless – factor is crucial. The self-analy-

3. *Creative Silence*, by Denis Duncan, 1980. Available from Ecclesia Services, One Cranbourne Road, London N10 2BT.

sis takes place in the presence of the utterly forgiving God. The divine presence – which, like Moses, Isaiah and so many of the Old Testament prophets, we approach with a sense of awe – is, in fact, on the authority of Jesus, the forgiving father. In the very moment of acknowledgement and repentance, the generosity and graciousness of God is active. So every aspect and consequence of our honest self-knowledge is embraced and encompassed in the knowledge we have of God as Jesus Christ revealed it. To those who say, with John Donne, 'But I have more', there comes simultaneously: 'My grace is sufficient for you'.

The search for other metaphors to describe the indescribable God must go on: metaphors relevant to our language, experience and culture. God is always contemporary, but whatever concepts are found, whatever images prove useful, they must never set aside that factor of personal relationship, marked by honesty on the human side and forgiving grace on the divine side. This is the essence of the divine–human encounter.

True religion, in the light of God's revelation in Jesus, must always be comforting, always encouraging, endlessly invigorating. That 'other Comforter', the living and abiding presence of Jesus, always brings power and creates strength. That message is, by derivation, within the word Comforter itself.

Spiritual Sterility

There are two negative, destructive factors, which were as evident to Jesus in his time as they are towards the end of this millennium. One is the closed mind, the other the hardening heart. The first is a denial of the ongoing creative activity of God. The second represents a declining spiritual sensitivity, which reduces our capacity to 'touch and handle things unseen'.

The closed mind restricts the possibility of growth intellectually, emotionally and spiritually. Openness to new aspects of understanding is not a threat to the foundations of faith, nor a denial that we have been given, through revelation and 'the Word of God', 'all that we need for our salvation'. Nor is it an invitation to rewrite the basic doctrines of the faith. It is an invitation to those who, secure in their religious convictions, want to learn more of the infinite wonder of a world created by a God whom we often tend to make (in J. B. Phillips' words) 'too small'.

The more sinister process is the hardening heart. The classic Old Testament example of this destructive development is the continual refusal of Pharaoh to let the children of Israel go, despite the sequence of plagues sent to him and his people. The repeated rendering of the phrase 'Pharaoh hardened his heart' underlines the subtle process of spiritual deterioration.

The ultimate result of the heart-hardening process is dramatically described by Jesus when he spoke of those who declared his demonstrations of divine power in healing miracles to be the work of Beelzebub, that is the Devil. When the heart is so hardened and the spirit is so sterile that the ability to distinguish between evil and good has been lost, spiritual sensitivity has become so low that the capacity for repentance must be nearly dead. And where there is no penitence, how can forgiveness be given? It is in the context of the hardening heart that Jesus speaks of the possibility of the unforgivable sin.

If there is spiritual sterility in our times, let this not be seen as a criticism applicable only to others. It is a confession of feelings we all share. The materialism expressed in the ruthlessness of market forces, the dominance of money in the problems of international relationships, the revolution in information technology and its influence on hidden persuasion, the dominant themes of everyday living – health, cosmetic improvement, invitation to greed – all this and more stifles the spirit, if we allow it to do so, and spiritual sensitivity declines.

The Church has many responsibilities – religious ordinances, social witness, prophetic proclamation, a concern for justice and reconciliation – but it must not forget that its primary task is the nurture of the spirit. Spiritual sensitivity and ruthless materialism cannot live together. It is imperative that the Church works to secure the triumph of the former over the latter and, as Paul wrote to Timothy, to 'fan into flame the gift of God'.

If Only . . .

'If only . . .' What feeling is contained in this simple phrase! Regret, remorse, sadness, self-criticism, guilt; so much lies behind the almost involuntary expression of these words. The feeling is always uncomfortable, always painful.

The actress Sylvia Read uses the phrase 'if only' a dozen times in rapid succession, as she wrestles with the horror of her son Jonathan's suicide at the age of 33. 'Those near to a dead friend or relative,' she writes in *Sharing a Grief* [4] 'are beset by "if only". In the days following Jonathan's suicide, I began unpicking days, weeks, years. There were so many things that perhaps could have been done differently, things that perhaps contributed to his death. The threads of the past got unpicked till they lay scattered all around me. The past was broken up in little pieces, and the pieces seemed to be pointing tiny hands at me and whispering "Guilty!" '

I was recently involved in a workshop at the residential weekend of The Compassionate Friends,* an organization which people join only for the saddest of reasons, namely that they have lost a child (at any age, and in whatever circumstances) through death. The purpose of the workshop was to help each other with the problems of anger and guilt. The commonest theme was the 'if only' one. Whatever the cause of death in each situation – road crash, illness, suicide – the pain was the guilt over believed failure to take some action that might have prevented that fatal situation arising. Many people have their own 'if only'.

I cannot find an example in Scripture of the literal use of these words in the sense that I am describing, but there is one situation in which they are, in effect, used. It occurs in John's Gospel (11:17-35). Lazarus had died three days previously, and although Jesus knew of his death, he decided not

4. *Sharing a Grief*, by Sylvia Read, Published by Ecclesia Services

to go immediately to Bethany, where Lazarus and his sisters Mary and Martha lived. When he did arrive, Martha said plaintively: 'If only you had come, my brother would not have died.' Jesus wept.

There are many reasons why that sense of remorse over things we believe we have failed to do in relation to someone who has died, will linger, perhaps for ever. In most cases, however, the reality is that we did what we could at the time; we are not omnipotent and may not have been able to act in a different way in the circumstances in which we feel we failed. It is so often only with hindsight that possible alternatives, if any, can be seen. To persist in 'unpicking the pieces' gives no benefit to those who have died and, in emphasizing guilty feelings to the point when they become inappropriate, we alone will be hurt.

It is particularly important for those with a religious faith to believe in the forgiveness of sins, for it is a primary doctrine of the Christian faith. It is in the infinite divine forgiveness that the failures of the past lose their power to hurt and to destroy – then we can move forward.

* a nationwide bereavement organisation for parents: 53 North Street, Bristol BS3 1EN

Holy Detachment

It is not money itself, but the love of it that is said to be the root of all evil. But there is much evil caused too by the extreme lack of money that genuine poverty represents. There are obvious links between unemployment and social misbehaviour, desperation and delinquency, destitution and depression, homelessness and hopelessness. Poverty as a vow, voluntarily made as an act of Christian obedience, is a noble virtue. But the poverty that is forced on people by social policy or political circumstance is another matter. Whether it is seen in our own society, through vast differences in the distribution of wealth, or at its horrific worst in underdeveloped parts of the world, concern for the needs of the poor represents a fundamental response inseparable from the demands of the gospel.

The Christian faith can never be other than a radical faith, rooting out whatever creates unacceptable inequality. The infinite value of every created being is built into the fabric of the Christian message. Equality may be an impossible aim, but equality of opportunity is not. Everyone must be given the chance to make the most of their creative potential, and any system which defeats that purpose deserves prophetic denunciation. To come to feel that money is of less and less importance is a sign of maturing spirituality. That is, of course, more easily said in comfortable financial circumstances than in dire straits. 'The best thing about getting old,' it has been said, 'is that all those things you couldn't have when you were young, you no longer want.'

That practical thought can be taken to a deeper level. 'Be not conformed to this world,' Paul wrote to the Ephesians, 'be ye transformed.' Growth in spirituality is demonstrated by the attitude we have to 'the world'. It is not that we grow away from involvement in this world, for no proper understanding of the doctrine of the Incarnation would allow that to happen. You are 'in the world', Jesus told his disciples. But he went on, 'You must not be *of* it'. Jesus shared the pain, the pressures, the suffering, the cruelty, the admiration, the criticism of the world as one who was 'truly human', but he demonstrates, for all the world to see and from it to learn, the vibrant concept of holy detachment. It does not mean leaving the world and its needs behind. Indeed, the greater the depth of true spirituality, the more will compassion for the world flow out. But it does involve finding the right relationship between the 'temporal' and the 'eternal', and between the kingdom and the 'other things'.

Holy detachment may be for most of us an experience of later life, but it needs to be a growing area for all.

Transformation

'One moment of ecstasy can transform your life.' The psychologist Margo Anand wrote this in relation to particular human experiences, but because the word 'ecstasy' relates to religious experiences too, the statement becomes important for spiritual development. In the university of life, there is a profound need for the transforming moment.

Ecstasy is (according to Professor E. J. Tinsley [5]) 'an overwhelming experience wherein the sense of individual selfhood is transcended, the primary tense dimensions of time, past, present and future are blended in an overwhelming sense of the eternal now and there is an unforgettable experience of serenity, well-being and joy'. Theoretical as that may sound, it nevertheless describes the experience of the saints and mystics – those who, as the spiritual writer Baron von Hügel testified, 'are never so fully active, so truly and intensely themselves, as when they are most truly possessed by God'.

Ecstasy, and the mysticism with which it is closely associated, lie outside the experience of most of us. Nor are they experiences that we can choose to achieve for they are gifts to be received gratefully and graciously. At the heart of them, however, is what everyone on the spiritual journey needs – an experience that is life-changing.

The biblical record contains many transforming experiences. When Moses came down from Mount Sinai with the tablets of stone, his face was 'radiant', as Aaron and all who were with him testified. Forty days and forty nights 'with the Lord' had clearly changed his life. The prophet Isaiah was moved to commitment because 'his eyes had seen the King'. St. Paul was 'caught up in Paradise' in a mystical

---

5. Article 'Ecstasy' by E. J. Tinsley, in *A Dictionary of Christian Theology*, edited by Alan Richardson, SCM, 1969.

experience, 'heard inexpressible things' and received 'surpassingly great revelations'. It was an experience that enabled him to learn of 'the grace that is sufficient'. For Jesus himself, the Transfiguration was such an experience, and we are told his face was 'shining like the sun'. The experience of the two who walked towards Emmaus and met the risen Lord must surely have found their lives transformed for ever.

The level of our spiritual life will be much less than the peak experiences of those of biblical times. But, then or now, the world is essentially the same. 'A garrulous and facile generation needs the mystic quiet' claimed a writer of the thirties. It could be a statement for today. In a world where charities ask for £2 a month to save a child while footballers are paid £40,000 a week; where a garrulous generation gossips over titillation and trivia; where a facile world fails to root out injustice, discrimination and abuse, the value of transforming personal experiences remains. It brings what C. S. Lewis describes as 'patches of Godlight in a sad, dark world'.

Transformation comes in many ways – through loving relationships, lively people, lasting memories, 'patches of Godlight'. In *The Merchant of Venice*, Portia declares, 'I have toward heaven breathed a secret vow to live in prayer and contemplation.' [6] To fulfil such a vow can only bring a blessing to this facile world.

6. Portia in *The Merchant of Venice*, Act III, scene iv.

Set Objectives

It can be disconcerting to lose touch with your roots, dangerous to remove your landmarks, disastrous not to determine your objectives. This somewhat alliterative sentence evolves out of reflection on two Old Testament passages. The first and third phrases come from the prophet Jeremiah, the middle statement from the Book of Proverbs. Roots, landmarks and goals are important.

The experience of losing your roots is emphasized by an image in Jeremiah 50:6. It is a pastoral one, common in the prophetic books: 'My people have been lost sheep . . . They wandered over mountain and hill, and forgot their own resting place.' That is indeed being lost. It is important for nations that they do not lose touch with their foundations; this makes the way that history is taught crucial. It is important that the Church thinks and acts 'in remembrance of Jesus'; that emphasizes the need for the traditional as well as the novel in worship and theology. It is important that as individuals we are aware of the people who have shaped us.

The loss of landmarks endangers the fabric of life. The words in Proverbs (23:10) no doubt refer to literal landmarks, but the metaphor is relevant to contemporary life. The intention of the proposed change to the Armed Services rule relating to the affairs members have with non-Service people (distinct from affairs between Service people, which will remain an offence) is not to lower standards and diminish values, but the current trends in relationship ethics cumulatively create a feeling of erosion that threatens the health of society. When traditional landmarks disappear, contemporary approaches to social and ethical problems (including the fields of both medical and Christian ethics) tend not to set up the markers that society needs and individuals miss. It is not universal immorality that is the danger for today, but a widespread amorality.

The ability to 'determine set objectives' is the mark of great statesmen – as R. A. Butler once pointed out in a reference to Ernest Bevin and Winston Churchill. It is a concept that meant much to a Church of Scotland minister for whom I have always had the greatest admiration and respect, the Revd John Brown, who died recently. He once preached a sermon on the Jeremiah passage to which I have referred. The exact text (Jeremiah 50:5) was: 'They will ask the way to Zion and turn their faces towards it'. Should not all of us determine set objectives, he asked? [7] (One of Mr Brown's sons is, significantly, the Chancellor, Gordon Brown.)

It was said of Jesus that he 'set his face steadfastly towards Jerusalem'. He had determined his objectives. The result is Christian history. His roots were in the Old Testament and the Jewish law. His landmarks were the commandments, both old and new. His purpose was the well-being, salvation, and wholeness of people. It is no wonder that his followers are asked to keep 'looking unto Jesus', for their roots, landmarks and objectives are in him.

7. *Gordon Brown, The Biography,* by Paul Routledge, Simon and Shuster, 1998.

Strengthen the Stakes!

What a wonderful resolution is to be found in the Old Testament prophet, Isaiah! If your vision is narrow; if your sense of adventure is diminishing; if your circle of interests is decreasing; if (as J. B. Phillips puts it) 'your God is too small', then listen to this:

Enlarge the place of your tent, stretch your tent curtains wide, do not hold back; lengthen your cords, strengthen your stakes. . . . Do not be afraid . . . (Isaiah 54:2, 4)

What could be a more stimulating and encouraging resolution than that?

The context relates to Israel's history but here let us simply reflect on the words themselves. If it is true that 'there's a wideness in God's mercy like the wideness of the sea'; if the characteristic of God's love is its 'length, breadth, depth and height', then our focus must be not on diminishment but on expansion; not on exclusiveness but on inclusiveness; not on negativism but on that which is positive. The characteristic of the divine love is not its restrictive boundaries, but its all-embracing essence. Enlarge, stretch, lengthen and strengthen. And have the faith to match!

When I was interviewed for a magazine article recently, one of the questions put to me was 'What causes you the most difficulty when it comes to believing in God?' I found myself spontaneously saying that it was encountering those who publicly and professionally claim to be God's servants, but who are totally lacking in humility, sensitivity and compassion. It is not so much the human failures or personal peccadilloes of which we are all guilty that are the real worry within the Church, but much more those unpleasant trends too frequently found there – small-mindedness, intolerance, petty jealousy, unwillingness to listen and consider, envy of position, arrogance in belief, impatience with weakness, blindness to goodness (the most serious sin of all, according to Jesus). If the Church is to proclaim the Gospel of love with conviction in a too-often unloving world, it must demonstrate its own ability to be a living, loving fellowship.

Those who saw the disciples fulfilling their ministry were impressed by the 'boldness' of their preaching, and the success of the healing miracle, but even more, it seems, by the radiance of spirit they expressed. The people 'took knowledge that they [the disciples] had been with Jesus'. Was there ever more telling testimony to the effect, albeit unconscious, on the life of the disciple?

Some may feel anxious that emphasizing expansion and enlargement may lead to a weakening of the faith; that inclusiveness implies the acceptance of fringe features; that there is danger in an over-liberal attitude; that the enlarged circle may not be as Christ-centred as it should be. But the theme contains the answer. If you enlarge and stretch and, in particular, lengthen the cords, *you must strengthen the stakes*. To be expanding and inclusive demands not less emphasis on basic beliefs, but more.

The firmer the foundations, the greater the expansion can be. The deeper the roots too, the taller is the tree.

The Silence of the Ears

'Love finds nothing to be glad about when someone goes wrong,' St. Paul tells the Corinthians, 'but is glad when truth is glad'. It is a text that needs to be writ large in every editorial and production office in the world of the media, for it condemns outright the exploitation of human failure for the sake of commercial gain as well as sensationalism, scandalmongering and the intimate gossip that is founded on rumour rather than fact. It would be naïve to expect the world of commercial communication to be governed by the principles of love, for circulation and viewing figures depend on much more worldly motives in an atmosphere of cut-throat competition. Bad news provides most of the news from around the world. However, there is a difference however between the recognition of that human fact and the deliberate and persistent pursuit of unhappy people who are victims of their own folly or others' failure, of being 'glad when someone goes wrong'. 'There but for the grace of God go I' is a necessary reminder of the universality of human weakness. We should be careful what we say about other people.

Mother Teresa, in her long life, often emphasized the importance of silence. 'We cannot put ourselves directly in the presence of God,' she once said, [8] 'if we do not practise internal and external silence.' On the significance of silence in personal life, she comments: 'Souls of prayer are souls of great silence'. Commending the silence 'which gives a new outlook on everything' she encourages the development of inner silence by practising the silence of the eyes, the silence of the ears, the silence of the tongue, the silence of the mind and the silence of the heart.

Consider Mother Teresa's concept of the silence of the ears. James, practical disciple that he was, made the neces-

8. *In the Heart of the World*, by Mother Teresa, New World Library, 1997.

sary point that we cannot do two contrary things together. He cites obvious examples. A fountain cannot gush with fresh and salt water at the same time. A fig tree cannot yield olives, nor a vine figs. It is a principle that holds good in the silence of the ears. Concentration on rumour, gossip and uncharitable words and other elements that (Mother Teresa again) 'come from fallen human nature', blots out the possibility of doing what those who serve God must do – listen. The prophet Elijah learned this lesson. The drama of earthquake, wind and fire deafened him to the still, small voice within. It was the necessary silence of the ears that enabled him to set aside despair and go back to the work he was called to do.

The silence of the ears will make those in search of their salvation listen to the voice of God within and the cry of the poor without. Only in silence can we learn the priorities of discipleship. Without such listening, discipleship will lose its purpose, and love for God and neighbour will be denied its full expression.

The Hermit's Way

'I rise at 3 a.m. for the office of Vigil at 3.30 a.m., returning to my hermitage thereafter for further devotions alone. Mass is at 6.30 a.m. followed immediately by a further hour of solitary prayer.' And so a normal day in the life of a hermitess unfolds. To read this programme of the holy life of a long-standing friend, formerly a specialist in her own professional field, compels respect and admiration. Hidden away on a holy island, inner happiness reigns. Is it escape from reality or a pilgrimage towards it?

Reading her letter takes me back to a visit last autumn to the village of Sachselm, near Lucerne in Switzerland. In the mountainous region east of the Lake of Sarnen, I visited the village of Flüeli. Nicklaus of Flüeli (peasant farmer, politician, magistrate, statesman, founder of Swiss unity and a creative originator of Swiss neutrality) lived in the fifteenth century, and was married to Dorothea, with whom he had ten children. He served on the town and cantonal councils and became a judge, yet, at the age of 50, and with the agreement of his wife, he took Jesus's words literally: 'No man is worthy of me who cares more for father or mother, son or daughter, than for me'. From that day he became Brother Klaus the hermit, living a disciplined life, sleeping on a bench or the bare floor, wearing a simple woollen cloak, using an old patched blanket on cold nights , until his death in 1487. The long path down to the hermitage in which those twenty years were spent is a journey through nature's splendour, a road now enjoyed by the streams of pilgrims who come to visit Brother Klaus's home. Not everyone will condone the fact the Brother Klaus left a family of ten children (however well-provided for materially), but the call to leave all and follow the hermit's life was crystal-clear to Brother Klaus.

Realistically, the kind of choice made by hermitess and hermit does not face many church members today. But it does remind us that the primary purpose of the Church is to provide the 'stabilizing power of the enduring spiritual realities'. The Church does not exist to fulfil social functions that are 'of less and less relevance to, or indistinguishable from, those carried out by secular institutions' says the spiritual writer, John Main. What a tragedy it is if the Church is so preoccupied with its problems, its image, its personnel, its structures, and its committees that it is not available to 'fan into flame the gift of God'. It is, or should be, a lively organism, firing up the holy life.

It is not a past experience that the Church exists to proclaim, but a present and powerful one. The risen Christ in its midst creates its stabilizing power today. The presently active Holy Spirit is dynamic power, the divine energy at work in the world. It is to that great reality the hermits bear witness by trying to practise what they preach.

The Pursuit of Simplicity

One of the less attractive features of modern life is its liking for jargon words that do not enhance the beauty of our language. The word 'downshifting' is certainly not an appealing one. The concept for which it stands should, however, engage our attention and fire our enthusiasm: it is that of voluntary simplicity.

I read with interest, surprise and pleasure that 'downshifting had become Britain's fastest growing lifestyle trend'. [9] There is no doubt that such a development will benefit the health of the nation, entangled as most of its citizens are in a very complicated world. Add the menace of materialism and the gargantuan problem of suffering in the world today when, as the hymn says, 'human hearts are breaking under sorrow's iron rod', and it is no wonder that stress and strain, anxiety and breakdown are hallmarks of our contemporary society. What a valuable concept voluntary simplicity is!

Religious folk should generally welcome the trend towards simplicity. Christians will feel it strikes a chord, for did not Jesus live the simple life? 'Foxes have holes and the birds their nests, but the Son of Man has nowhere to lay his head.' He had no property, no bank accounts, no mortgages, no hire-purchase agreements, no credit cards. His was (in material terms) a simple life, but it was a simplicity that was entirely voluntary. Should not the disciple seek to reflect the Master?

The simple life is, of course, still lived in religious communities where poverty, chastity and obedience are life-long vows. Voluntary simplicity goes even further in the case of a nun I know who lives the life of a hermit. She tells me that the main features of the eremitical life are 'frugality, silence,

---

9. From 'Back to Basics' by Michael Green, quoted in *Ethos, The Ethics in Business Magazine*, August–September 1997.

solitude and simplicity'. The life of prayer to which the hermit is called, she says, 'requires a quiet, regular pace of life, conducive to recollection, guarding the imagination, avoiding the kind of external activity that could interfere with devotion'. Few can pursue the hermit's life, but what she says about it can surely be translated into a voluntary simplicity which, to embrace, would in itself be an act of dedication or rededication.

Voluntary simplicity involves, as some see it, a retreat to rural places and natural conditions, but it does not have to take that shape. Many will have to work out the meaning of voluntary simplicity in suburbia, industrial towns or cities. Voluntary simplicty does not mean seeking an escape or dropping out. It is an act of obedience. 'Simplicity of living means meeting life face to face . . . without unnecessary distractions, without trying to soften the awesomeness of our existence or mask the deeper significance of life with pretentious, distracting and unnecessary accumulations . . . It results in a more fulfilled and richer life that is not dictated by debt, junk and that never-ending quest for status and position'. [10]

To change our way of life drastically demands a major effort of will – and faith. But it could be profoundly worthwhile, to diligently seek such voluntary simplicity. Or, less attractively, downshifting.

10. *The Voluntary Society*, by Duane Elgin.

Inner Resources

It would not be surprising if counselling agencies, psychotherapy clinics, psychiatric departments in hospitals and, not least, doctors' surgeries find themselves under pressure at this time. If this is so, it will not only be because it is the season for winter ills and 'blues'. It concerns the possibility of post-millennial deflation and depression, and this is related to very basic psychological and spiritual realities.

The millennial experience was, individually and corporately, a memorable one. The splendour of the televised displays on the River Thames in London, the Eiffel Tower in Paris, Princes Street in Edinburgh, City Square in Belfast, and countless other places around the world, brought elation and excitement to millions. The services in cathedrals in London, Edinburgh and Belfast, and the outstanding *Songs of Praise* from the Millennium Stadium in Cardiff (where 66,000 people were present), paid a triumphant tribute to the religious significance of the event. Words of hope and encouragement; messages about compassion and service; exhortations commending new beginnings and new opportunities – altogether a high level of excitement was created, making a unique occasion (in an individual life) an unforgettable one.

Then life has to return to 'normal'. The human spirit cannot remain at a perpetual psychological or spiritual peak; reality, with its stress and struggle, grief and sadness, fear and frustration, pain and suffering, is there as it always is. The post-millennial experience may portray, in an acute form, the alternation so often present between elation and depression, ecstasy and desperation.

Mood swings are part of being human. It is simply part of our common experience that we can, on occasion, reach the heights of spiritual experience and for various reasons (traumatic events, combinations of negative circumstances, relationship crises, etc.) touch rock bottom.

The variation in moods and the alternating of elation and despair in the flow of life need not lead us to despair. The important part is to recognize the reality of our temperamental and spiritual frailty. If caught up in negative feelings such as these, there are three directions in which help lies. The first is the importance of the will to change attitudes. Depression is, by definition, not something that can be cured by act of will, but the attitude we take to the situation in which we find ourselves is important. The second is to seek help from a pastoral adviser, spiritual director, therapist or counsellor, creating a context in which fears and feelings can be looked at in safety. The third is to realize anew 'the grace that is sufficient for all our needs'. 'I have learned to find resources in myself whatever the circumstances', St. Paul wrote to the Philippians. Within religious faith, the means of grace are always there, and the reality of the power of the Holy Spirit to change and renew can be acknowledged.

The Power of Love

The congregation was singing the traditional prayer 'Make me a channel of our peace', sometimes attributed to St. Francis. It contains the words: 'Master, grant that I may never seek so much to be consoled as to console'. To my later horror, I was heard by my neighbour to sing (though I knew it not) '. . . never seek so much to be controlled as to control'. It was a Freudian slip, but a worrying one.

A desire for power lies deep within the unconscious of many of those who are called to leadership, despite Lord Acton's well-known warning: 'All power corrupts and absolute power corrupts absolutely'.

The contemporary theologian, Sally McFague, writes in *Models of God* [11]: 'At the heart of all the issues, the nuclear issue and issues of political and social oppression, is the question of power. Who wields it? Of what sort is it?' It is a personal issue too – and always has been. The source of the cardinal sin which brought expulsion from the Garden of Eden for our archetypal ancestors, Adam and Eve, was the desire for power. They sought to be 'as gods'.

The question of power, and how it is incarnated in individuals and corporate groups, lies at the root of many problems: in politics, be it in a democracy or a dictatorship; in economics, especially in the abuse of wealth; in media control and ownership; in the Church, which has its own 'corridors of power'; in professional relationships - therapeutic, psychiatric, medical, analytical; with the mass media-backed evangelist, exorcist or 'healer'. 'The greater the power, the more dangerous the abuse,' warns Edmund Burke.*

Religion is not wholly helpful in guiding us on issues of power. In the biblical story of creation, man and woman are

---

11. *Models of God,* by Sally McFague, SCM Press, 1987.

given 'dominion' over birds, beasts, fish and 'every creeping thing', but, as recent incidents have again shown, that power can be abused. A great deal of the language of the Old Testament is expressed in images of power and subservience, where concepts such as kingship and lordship are used as models of the divine–human relationship. That is one of the reasons why contemporary theologians search for other models and metaphors more meaningful to modern believers. The liturgical language of public prayer employs a term such as 'almighty Father' which, on reflection, seems self-contradictory. Do 'almighty power' and the 'divine love' revealed in Jesus, sit comfortably together?

'The love of power,' wrote William Hazlitt 'is the love of ourselves'. ** It is that which concerns me over my Freudian slip. If we possess, personally or in some corporate context, the privilege of power, it must be expressed in terms of outgoing love to God and neighbour. 'All power is given to me in heaven and in earth', said Jesus after his resurrection. Power is only in safe hands when it belongs to 'love incarnate, love divine'. To have the privilege of power is therefore to need the gift of grace. Only then will it be expressed, not in domination, but in love.

* Speech in the Middlesex Elections, February 1771.
** *Political Essays*, 1819.

Tears of Compassion

Jesus not infrequently accused his disciples of having 'little faith' and criticized their failure to believe that 'the things which are impossible with men are possible with God', that 'with God all things are possible'. But are they? The human dilemma is the conflict between an obedient desire to believe in divine omnipotence and the harsh realities of life experienced in natural disaster, murder, accident or any other of the forms of human suffering that tie faith in knots.

For a very specific declaration of the omnipotence of God, turn to Genesis and Sarah, Abraham's wife. The promise of a child in her old age by a centenarian husband was too much for her mind or even her imagination. Her response was laughter. It was through Abraham that God conveyed a rebuke for such a lack of faith with the clearly rhetorical question: 'Is anything too hard for the Lord?'

Is it? Those bereaved in Turkey's earthquake, the broken-hearted parents who have lost a child, the cancer victims facing terminal illness, may all find it hard to give the expected answer. Despite faith, prayer, perhaps lifelong commitment and obedience, the sought-for deliverance has not come. Was this because God did not so will it? Was it because there are some things God cannot do?

Those who ridicule religious faith by pointing to massive human suffering, corporate or personal, always ask how a loving God can permit such suffering. That accusation will continue. What is more trying is the profound crisis of faith and doubt that suffering can (though does not always) bring to the genuine believer, brought up to accept words of authority which claim that nothing is too hard for the Lord (as God told Abraham), and that with God all things are possible (as Jesus told the world).

Having given the gift of free will and freedom to human beings, God is bound by the gift and cannot necessarily prevent the results of that freedom. If human freedom is a reality, human suffering is an inevitable consequence. Those with faith will, however, see the providential presence of God in the way human situations develop. There is no doubt that, in the deliverance of the Israelites at the Red Sea, it was in just such a way that the event was interpreted for the eternal importance of Israel's history. Divine synchronicity can say something very important through suffering and many will bear personal testimony to such experience.

When Jesus wept over Jerusalem, it was the irony of what he could have done, but was not allowed to do, which caused his tears. There are some things that are 'too hard', even for God. Disaster, be it naturally caused or through human failing – or a combination of both – leaves us with the mystery of suffering unsolved. It was not, however, frustration alone that made Jesus cry. He also felt profound compassion. Here is a glorious paradox! It is from the deep wells of human suffering that compassion freely flows.

II. Seeds of Renewal

1) Ashes

2) *

Healthy Hilarity

*

It was exhilarating to read some words from Genesis this morning. 'God has brought me laughter', said Abraham's wife, Sarah. And that laughter would have been infectious, for she added 'everyone who hears about this will laugh with me!' The reason for such hilarity? That God had promised Sarah, 'well-advanced in years' and 'past the age of childbearing', a son by her centenarian husband! So she laughed when the promise was made (and felt some guilt about it too!), and she laughed when Isaac was born.*

Sadly this world seems to be, for many, less a joyous journey and more a vale of tears. There has been human suffering beyond comprehension through the conflict in the Balkans [12]. To the cry 'Lord, how long?', there is no answer when starvation stalks the earth. The cruel hurricane, the devastating flood, the destructive earthquake, are all headlines for a day, only to be forced off the front pages – and therefore away from our attention – by the trivialities of celebrities' relationships and sporting controversies. So often it is ill-health and death that seem to dominate life, as the telephone brings news of another cancer victim amongst our friends, an approaching death amongst our relatives, or a crippling marital conflict. Against such a background, the God-given laughter of Sarah is indeed exhilarating. It reminds us of the wonder of the joy, the divine surprise and the new beginnings that brought her such glee.

In the splendid hymn by Richard Gillard, 'Brother, sister, let me serve you', he writes: I will weep when you are weeping, when you laugh, I'll laugh with you; I will share your joy and sorrow till we've seen this journey through.

Pastoral responsibility for those for whom life is bleak and blighted, tense and tragic, is deeply embedded in religious faith. But it is equally important that Christianity proclaims the wonder inherent in being human. Within the divine creation, there was provided the capacity for goodness, creativity, inspiration, wonder and love. The Spirit of God which, in the creation story 'hovered over the waters', becomes, in the Christian story, the energizing Holy Spirit at work in the world and in human beings.

So where that Spirit is at work, 'fruits of the Spirit' will evolve in glorious splendour – love, joy, peace, patience, kindness, goodness, faithfulness, gentleness and self-control. Against these things (Paul writes to the Galatians), 'there is no law'. Indeed, there is everything to be said for them!

There is a time to weep and weep we will – with others, for others, alone. But thanks to Sarah and her joyous glee, we are reminded that there is a time to laugh and laugh we must. Health is helped by genuine hilarity. It is, as Sarah said, a gift from God.

* This incident is also referred to in Meditation Number 17.

With Respect

The poet proclaims it, the Psalmist sings it. 'The world is charged with the grandeur of God', writes Gerard Manley Hopkins. 'The heavens declare the glory of God and the firmament sheweth his handywork', exclaims the author of an Old Testament psalm. We all surely share a sense of wonder when we ponder creation. Yet that which was made so good is so spoiled that Wordsworth can say with sadness (in his 'Ode on the Intimations of Immortality'): 'But yet I know, where'er I go, there hath passed a glory from the earth'. The headlines of yesterday, of today and no doubt of tomorrow bear witness to that decline.

In religious terms, sin is to blame for the descent from grandeur to departed glory. A fundamental arrogance, expressed in a lack of respect for the Creator, was the reason why Adam and Eve were ejected from the Garden of Eden. They wanted to be 'as gods'. In cultural terms, that attitude is expressed as a process of secularization with denial of the spiritual dimension and the assumption of power by human beings.

A lack of respect characterizes many contemporary attitudes, personal and corporate. Many organizations for the disabled feel that current legislation benefits not the service-user but the service-provider denying respect to people with disabilities. Trivial increases to the State pension do not respect people who have contributed, often notably, to the welfare of the community and nation. All respect for the sacred intimacies of relationships has been jettisoned by a society that disconnects sex and love and believes 'anything goes'. And (while recognizing that it is the sin of the few, not the many) the increasing incidence of paedophilia demonstrates a total lack of respect for the 'little ones' who must not be offended. All this adds up to an arrogance that changes the Psalmist's words from 'What is man that thou art mindful of him?' to 'What is God that we should be mindful of him?' The process of secularization leads, as Thomas Oden, the American theologian and psychotherapist claims [13], to 'the reduction of human existence to spiritless body, sexuality to depersonalized orgasm, sciences to amoral data-gathering and politics to the manipulation of power, systematically ignoring the human capacity for transcendence, moral reasoning and self-sacrificial love'.

Worship is essentially reverential adoration, in other words respect for God. 'The idea of the holy' is a mystery that has been recognized down the ages by prophets and priests, saints and sinners. We simply do not live by bread alone. The human mind is forever reaching out for the knowledge that is beyond knowledge. The human spirit yearns for the divine embrace expressed in a love that will not let us go. To lose all awareness of the great mystery, to lack the imagination and the intuition that can sense the presence of the eternal, to miss the signs and wonders of the Spirit is to lose that 'good part' which Mary of Bethany chose to learn as she sat at Jesus's feet.

13. Thomas Oden quoted in *The Risks of Freedom*, published by The Pastoral Care Foundation in the Philippines, 1993.

Out of the Dump

It is not surprising that the Jesus who came 'down to earth' (this is what the creeds call the Incarnation) was strikingly practical in spiritual matters. That was certainly true of his dealings with his disciples during his life, but the same 'down to earthness' is shown in what he said to them after his resurrection. To bemused followers, asking if the time was at hand 'to restore the kingdom to Israel', he dismissed the disciples' irrelevant question with a reminder that it was not for them 'to know the times and dates', which are God's business, but rather to point them to immediate, practical priorities – to get on with the work of the kingdom through preaching the gospel bequeathed to them.

Still bemused by Jesus's ascension, the disciples stood 'gazing up into heaven'. The theme of practicality was then taken up by 'two men in white' suddenly standing by them. Their rebuke is peremptory as they make it clear that this is no time for impractical puzzlement and wonder. 'Why do you stand gazing up into heaven?' they ask. Jesus will return, in due time, but in the meantime, action is needed. As Margaret Silf has put it: 'If we look for signs in the heavens, we may easily overlook God's footprints in the High Street' [14]. It is time for the disciples to be down to earth and get on with the Lord's business.

The practice of the awareness of the presence of God, the development of the devotional life and the creation of true spirituality depend on means of inner growth such as meditation, contemplation and, for those so favoured with the gift, mystic exhilaration. We must touch and handle things unseen. But spirituality is not mere evanescent spiritual excitement. It is the down-to-earth love that will not let people go, that lifts human beings 'out of the dump'.

14. *Taste and See: Adventuring into Prayer*, by Margaret Silf, Darton, Longman & Todd.

That last phrase is the title of a book of remarkable photographs taken in Guatemala City. Its cover picture is of three lovely, lively little girls, smiling and serene. They have been rescued from the rubbish dump in that city where some 1,500 people 'live', most of them children who struggle to collect cardboard, plastic, glass – indeed anything that can be recycled. They scavenge for bits of food to eat and items to resell. An American photographer, Nancy McGirr, was photographing the dump and its inhabitants when she became aware of the children's interest in cameras and decided to create a project whereby she takes small groups of children and teaches them a marketable skill that will help lift the next generation 'out of the dump'. The book is the result.

There is a part of our spirituality which relates to heavenly things, but it only becomes mature when it is expressed in the High Street, the rubbish dumps, the places where human need is greatest. It is part of true spirituality to be able to descend into hell, in Jesus's name.

Out of the Ashes

The moving and exciting final item in Walt Disney's *Fantasia 2000* is Stravinsky's ballet music, *The Firebird*. Presented as it was on 'the largest screen in Europe' [15] some 18 m (60 ft) high, the impact of the images accompanying the music is dramatic indeed. In this myth, the theme is 'life, death and renewal'. That is a sequence familiar in other areas of life. We see it annually in nature's seasons. We have it specifically in the great Christian themes of life, crucifixion and resurrection. It is a stimulating, encouraging theme because in each instance the end of it is triumph.

The symbol of fire is hugely present in the Bible. Fire can, as it did in The Firebird, bring devastating destruction, but it is also a symbol of God's presence in the story of Moses and the burning bush, a symbol of God's providential companionship on the journey through the desert when the children of Israel were guided by a 'pillar of fire' and a symbol of the cleansing, renewing Spirit of God at the first Pentecost. Charles Wesley sings about the place of fire in the renewal of life when he writes: 'O thou who camest from above, the pure celestial fire to impart, kindle a flame of sacred love on the mean altar of my heart. There let it for thy glory burn with inextinguishable blaze'.

If renewing fire is seen to have a part in reviving and redirecting the mission of the Church, its destructive aspect should be recognized and respected. Radical renewal and reformation demand the letting go and leaving behind of cherished but irrelevant attitudes, familiar but faulty ways and established but out-of-date habits. But that process must never be allowed to go too far and all the glorious benefits of the past be lost for ever. The Benedictine nun, Joan Chittester, while pleading for disciples to 'turn into fire'

15. IMAC Cinema, Waterloo, London.

also helpfully defines the role of the fire in the ashes in her illuminating book [16]. She does this with the help of the term 'grieshog'. Gaelic speakers tell us that grieshog is the process of burying warm coals in ashes at night in order to preserve the fire for the cold morning to come. The previous day's glowing coals were preserved under beds of ash so that a fire could be kindled quickly the next day. The old fire did not die; it kept its heat in order to be prepared to light the new one.

It is the great combination of a proper assessment of past values, and an adventurous risk-taking in the future, that brings fire from under the ashes. Language, concepts, and images tied to the past may have to be consumed, but the fundamental convictions founded on the One who is the same yesterday and forever, buried in the ashes will, when fanned into flame by the Spirit, bring the 'celestial fire' so essential for a needy world.

16. *The Fire in These Ashes,* by Joan Chittester, Gracewing, 1997.

Let Us All Pray

'There are diversities of gifts, but the same Spirit is the source of all of them.' The laying down of that principle by Paul, in his letter to the Corinthian church about errors in its life, spelt out for them the important relationship between unity and variety. On the core of the faith, every member of the Christian community must unite. He sums up that core as the confession 'Jesus is Lord'. The 'deep roots and firm foundation' established, there is room for all kinds of difference in the ways individuals express their beliefs in action, in the gifts that they have, in the ways that they serve. Temperaments vary. The extrovert personality can express itself in a heartiness that the reserved find impossible. The intellectual will philosophize about belief in an articulate manner in a way that is different from the 'simple faith' of many believers. But one is not 'right' and the other 'wrong'. It is only a matter of legitimate variation.

The kind of worship that brings benefit to people varies from one church member to another. For some, the dignity of the ordered liturgy of the Book of Common Prayer is essential; for others informal, unstructured worship ministers to their spiritual life. Others may want the moving silence of the Quakers. Some will feel their worship needs cannot be met without participation in the Mass. Such variations are not unhealthy. What is unhealthy is any dogmatic attitude that arrogantly proclaims any approach other than its own to be unacceptable. Difference is not a threat where the bases of faith are sound.

It is for similar reasons that different forms of renewal should be welcomed. Movements for liturgical renewal can have profound effects on the spiritual life of worshippers. Forms of charismatic renewal with a proper emphasis on the renewing power of the Spirit have brought new inspiration to some people. Evangelistic crusades and missions aimed at a clear, direct offering of the grace of the gospel, have brought many to a lifelong commitment to discipleship. Whatever is done 'decently and in good order' to renew spiritual life is to be welcomed rather than criticized.

Billy Graham's visit to Glasgow in the sixties had its effect on my congregation in the east end of the city. That influence was not expressed in an influx of new Christians who had 'gone forward' at the Kelvin Hall, for I cannot remember even one such addition. What I do recall is that the effect on the young people already in the church was profound. They were noticeably drawn to a much deeper level of faith by the experience of the crusade. As a result, my youth fellowship produced three ordained ministers, two deaconesses, one (as it was then called) missionary to Africa, and several long-serving elders in their various congregations.

'Come, Holy Spirit, come', we pray in expectation. That coming may be in diverse forms. It is not, however, the means through which that coming is expressed that is important, but the end result, namely growth in grace.

Shafts of Light

I have received an unusual gift. It is a table lamp with a shade that is open at the top, in a very heavy blue paper; the word 'light' is visible when it is not switched on. But when it is turned on, the change is dramatic. There, in white lettering, are the very first verses of the Bible: 'And darkness was on the face of the deep', it reads. 'God said: "Let there be light", and there was light.'

How one wishes that it was so easy in real life! Flick the switch and the darkness is dispelled! One touch and all around us is light. How wonderful it would be if a miracle – be it medical, psychological, emotional or spiritual – would follow at the flick of a switch. But in reality there is seldom a miracle for those for whom that darkness is all too real. Those feelings of darkness, depression, despair, doubt, even desperation, can be all too persistent.

The world is, of course, not a wholly negative place with most of life lived out in the shadows. There are many good people, positive happenings and creative developments in the world. But equally for many the darkness is all too real. Doctors' surgeries have many who are there not for physical reasons but because of anxiety and fear. Many hospital beds are occupied by those who are suffering nervous strain. In our own circles, many in our family, church or leisure groups are victims of some illness. Darkness and despair seem to abound. Sometimes that leads, at its worst, to suicide, the incidence of which is rising, especially among young men. More often it is expressed in depression – that sense of being weighed down with anxiety, a fear of not being able to cope, a reluctance to face a new day. Are there shafts of light to help us to break up such darkness? Perhaps there are.

The first is the usefulness of healthy self-awareness, of trying to understand just why our moods can change and what particularly pulls us down. The second is the other

51

side of that advice. Concern with self, if it is too continuous and concentrated, can create anxiety and fear. But fear is at the other end of the spectrum from love for (says St. John), 'perfect love casts out fear'. The more we are involved in love for others, the less we will be involved in unhealthy self-concern.

Thirdly, at the heart of faith is the theme of death and resurrection, the ability to learn to live again. Let me not make this point by way of platitude or theory, but rather direct you to people – you know them, as I do – who have faced, through accident or disability, a living death but who are examples of true resurrection, people who bring us a shaft of glorious light against the background of their own personal darkness. They are the ones who teach us how to learn to live again.

One-step Dance

To have a grand aim is a proper part of creative living. St. Paul spoke of his sense of purpose: 'Forgetting those things which are behind and reaching forth to the things which are before,' he said 'I press toward the mark for the prize of the high calling of God in Christ Jesus'. To have goals, to set aims and pursue ideals is to have a positive attitude to life. It has often resulted in great achievements.

What is true in general may, however, bring problems in particular situations. Those who are lost in the darkness of depression and despair, for example, simply cannot cope with exhortations to 'look forward'. Those who have suffered a bereavement – especially if it is a tragic one such as the death of a child, the suicide of a teenage son or daughter, the murder of a member of the family – just cannot contemplate the distant future. All they can do is try to cope with the dreadful present.

Ponder four statements which, broadly speaking, have a common theme. The first comes from Edmund Burke: 'Nobody made a greater mistake than he (she) who did nothing because they could do only a little.' The second is attributed to Madame du Deffand: 'The distance is nothing. It is only the first step that is difficult.' The third was the spontaneous reaction of astronaut Neil Armstrong to walking on the moon: 'That is one small step for a man, but a giant leap for mankind.' The fourth comes from John Henry Newman's hymn 'Lead, kindly light': 'I do not ask to see the distant scene, one step enough for me.' They all underline the importance of one step.

There are several contexts in which taking one step is extraordinarily difficult but extremely important. There is, for example, the situation where someone needs counselling and that step is the crucial one of lifting a telephone to say 'I need help. Can I have an appointment?' There is the evangelical one in which resistance to the first necessary step of making a commitment obstructs the act of confession and faith. But it is in the field of bereavement, particularly, that progress (if it is possible at all) must be in the form of one step at a time. To take one pace towards coping, towards growth, can make severe demands on those so bereft that they feel they have no future at all.

To become a partner with someone in grief or pain, darkness or despair, is to engage in that one-step dance that encourages healing. But the image needs qualification. A one-step dance is a rapid succession of quick steps. That could, alas, be well beyond the capacity of the wounded and the hurt. It is the very essence of the healing relationship to be acutely sensitive to the pace which the bereaved and the depressed can accept, and to recognize that the very most that can be faced is one step at a time.

Darkness, My Friend

No matter how often you read the Bible, a verse, a text or a passage can still strike you as completely new. It may be because of its relevance at that particular time and in that particular place, or some psalm of praise reflects your joy, some word of encouragement meets a need, or some anguished cry touches your own pain. It happened like that yesterday.

It is part of the pastor's life to encounter the pain and anguish of his or her people. It may be, as last weekend, a plea to 'please pray for my parish priest for his father has an inoperable cancer'. The condition is, sadly, not unusual but the particular circumstances made it poignant. It may be the letter that came a few days ago from 'friends of a friend'. Their 11-year-old daughter died in an horrific home accident four years ago, and now their 20-year-old son has died from Sudden Death Syndrome.

But back to the passage that I happened to read yesterday. It was Psalm 88, a psalm of anguish that ended (in the New International Version) with the compelling cry: 'The darkness is my closest friend'. How descriptive this is of the anguish experienced by priest and parents. On this psalm of loss and bereavement, the loss of friends and the absence of God, one commentator writes: 'Psalm 88 is the utterance of one who, in unrelieved anguish, "cleaves to God most passionately when God seems to have withdrawn himself most completely". You have taken my companions and my loved ones from me: the darkness is my closest friend'. Such anguish!

Anguish involves the feeling that 'whatever you thought was the beneficent power of creation is a childish error . . . so that, finally, you give up hope and say there is nothing positive in life whatever'. Dr Martin Israel, pathologist, priest and a long-time friend, wrote these words from his own experience of deep depression (described in his book *Dark Victory* [17]) and more recently, of the sheer physical weakness that led him towards near-death. In his later book (*Doubt, the Way of Growth* [18]), he writes of the necessity of suffering anguish. 'Until you have experienced anguish, you have not lived a full, proper life.' That is something that can only be said by one who has suffered greatly and come to see that somewhere within the suffering there can be a hint of light.

A theatre visit this same week movingly underlined the anguish of suffering. My old friends, Sylvia Read and William Fry present *Shadowlands* [19], in which C. S. Lewis's faith struggles with the fact of his wife's terminal cancer. It is not wrong to rail against the injustice of such suffering, but thanks be to those who, like John Milton in his blindness, see in the darkness a glimpse of light. 'So by this infirmity,' he wrote, 'may I be perfected, by this completed. So by this darkness, may I be enclosed in light.' Darkness, my friend!

17. *Dark Victory*, by Dr Martin Israel, Mowbray, 1995.

18. *Doubt, the Way of Growth*, by Dr Martin Israel, Mowbray, 1997.

19. Performed by Theatre Roundabout, 859 Finchley Road, London NW11 8LX.

Spiritual Gifts

The coming of the Holy Spirit at the first Pentecost was a dramatic and exciting happening. The imagery described in that story – rushing wind and tongues of fire – enhances the sense of mystery. The behaviour of the apostles was wrongly interpreted by puzzled observers as drunkenness, but there was no disorder among the disciples. Indeed Peter, as their accepted leader, delivered a clear and coherent description of the significance of what was happening, rooting it in the Old Testament scripture and offering an impromptu declaration of the meaning of the event in relation to Christ, crucified and risen.

These characteristics of order and coherence are important in assessing the validity and value of contemporary expressions of what are claimed to be movements of the Spirit. Many have found help in what has been described as 'the Toronto Blessing', for example, but features of that experience are not justified by Scripture. This is not to deny the element of renewal in the Toronto Blessing, but to ensure that any movements of renewal must be tested against Scripture and by their fruits.

The question of speaking in tongues, seen as a manifestation of the Spirit's activity, had created difficulties in the Corinthian church. Paul did not deny the validity of speaking in tongues as a spiritual gift, but he did minimize its importance among the range of gifts. He compares speaking in tongues unfavourably with prophecy. There seems too to have been some disorder created in that church by the abuse of speaking in tongues.

Paul is concerned to establish two principles. The first is that the Spirit creates not disorder but order, and the second is the importance of intelligibility. Neither disorder nor unintelligibility are for the edification of the church. He therefore recommends that when speaking in tongues takes place, there must be someone there who is able to interpret. If that condition is not met, what is being said brings no benefit to the community and really becomes a form of spiritual self-indulgence.

Paul seeks to emphasize the communal nature of the faith. While the need for personal decision on central matters of belief must always be recognized, it is important that the corporate nature of the church is understood. Whatever gifts we have, such as the gift of healing, must be used *within* the body of Christ and for the benefit of the whole church. If a healing gift exists in someone, that gift should be tested and, once recognized by the church, should be used within it as a contribution to its total ministry.

It is no accident that it is in this context Paul proclaims (in I Corinthians 13) the centrality of love. Love is the guiding principle in every aspect of the church's life and work. If that principle abounds, no one in the church will use any aspect of its life for selfish purposes, even if genuine spiritual gifts are involved. Whatever is done must be done to the glory of God and be a blessing to people.

Vocabulary of Love

There is a curious comment in W. H. Auden's poem on the death of W. B. Yeats. 'Poetry makes nothing happen', he writes. Can this be so? Because poetry is the literary form that uses the imagination allied to the harmony of words, it surely is capable of 'moving' someone and indeed of moving them on. From the huge range of poets from every age and place, we choose our favourites, a choice almost certainly based on the poets' capacity to encourage, challenge, inspire or change us.

That capacity to develop us in profound ways is shared with other literary forms. The play, the novel and the film has as its primary purpose our entertainment, but the playwright, the film-maker and the novelist can also bring a crusading element to their work. That is likely to be implicit rather than explicit, subtle rather than patent, but it is the factor that may make things happen by presenting new perspectives on old problems, and critical analyses of public attitudes and mores.

It is the purpose of religion to bring about change in the human condition, both at a personal and a social level. The Old Testament and the New Testament both encourage repentance and the renunciation of past weakness, and exhort men and women to renew their commitment to obedience to God – that is to raise the level of their spiritual awareness. But the means of achieving this aim is almost always a book. The Christian faith, like the Jewish faith, has its Word of God and the function of that literary work (which includes history, poetry, parable and drama) is to make things happen in the lives of people. 'The sword of the Spirit which is the Word of God' is, in St. Paul's view, an essential element in any campaign to bring about change.

If change, conversion and renewal are to take place, they must touch the 'inward parts' of our being. In more contemporary language, that means that to be effective, change must happen at the unconscious level of our personality and being. Unless 'deep speaks to deep', unless grace touches the parts beyond the reach of human systems of education or philosophy, the miracle of interior change will not take place. The turning-point in spiritual renewal comes when both conscious and unconscious levels are touched by grace. Then things happen.

Mother Teresa talked of 'a vocabulary of love'. She was not thinking only of the power of words – in poetry or any other literary form – though she used them to great effect in changing attitudes. The vocabulary of love is words in action. However much her words struck home at all levels of society, it was the vocabulary of love incarnate in action which so influenced the world – the multitude of hospitals, clinics, orphanages, hospices that she created. The greatest effect of all in 'making things happen' remains the life of the servant of God who is a vocabulary of love incarnate.

Real Change

Changed people change situations (I wrote recently). They
do. Things begin to happen when change takes place not
only in the minds of people but in their hearts; when it
affects their inner being, when it reaches 'the unconscious'.
Why then do so many people believe that, for some people
and some situations, change is impossible? The arrogance
with which so many commentators and critics dismissed the
reality of the conversion of the recently executed American
murderess, even though they had no personal contact with
her, is disturbing. Guards who were in continuous contact
with her, who acknowledged that Death Row conversions
are often (perhaps usually) insincere, opportunist or manip-
ulative, testified that in this case the change was real and
total; yet distant observers dismiss the possibility of change!
Of course it does not alter her guilt or the need for some
punishment, but the change was manifestly real.

The evidence of change is in the difference it makes to
attitudes, temperament, actions, relationships and life. Such
change was there for opponents and critics to see when the
despised tax-gatherer, Zacchaeus, emerged from his private
encounter with Jesus and issued a public apology (which
must have been desperately hard to make), backing it up by
righting situations that were the result of his past actions.
There were those who were 'baffled' by the preacher Paul
in Damascus (Acts 9:21): 'Isn't he the man who caused
havoc in Jerusalem among those who call on this name?' It
seems to be difficult for so many to believe in the possibility
of genuine change. But the positive proof is in the changed
situations that follow. How glorious is the witness of those
who, because their lives have been transformed, set out to
change the world and its ways.

Jesus spoke about the nature of change – or conversion
– in the parable of the sower. The seed that falls on rocky

61

ground finds poor, shallow soil and so the plant withers. The same thing happens when change is superficial and does not reach the deep places. New life simply dies. The seed that lands among thorns is choked and destroyed. So it is with the superficial conversion that is undermined by the pleasures and material attractions of the world. Only the seed that falls on good ground flourishes, for its roots can spread. Likewise, conversion is complete when it moves on to total commitment, when change brings fruit of some kind. Conversion is real when it embraces the unconscious as well as the conscious, when it touches the heart as well as the mind.

To be able to judge when change is real is not easy. To be glad when it is demonstrated is to reflect the joy felt over the prodigal son: he 'was dead and is alive again'. To deny it is to join with the thoroughly virtuous but stubborn elder brother who could not believe that his brother had changed. He had! His father certainly knew it. The right response to profound change for the better is not half-hearted hesitancy or cynical condemnation. It must be 'Hallelujah!'

Inner Vision

That politicians, like policemen, seem to be getting younger may be a sign of advancing years! The fact that there are young men and women in high office is, nevertheless, a trend not to be discouraged. The President of the United States, the last Prime Minister, the present Prime Minister and the Chancellor of the Exchequer are all men of youthful vigour. When that is combined with vision, it should be a healthy combination. This year's General Election [20] produced a plethora of youthful parliamentarians. They may lack experience, but they bring awareness of the attitudes and ideals of younger generations. If they can learn quickly (and there is nothing like heavy public responsibility to encourage that process), they can bring into politics not only the traditional 'breath of fresh air', but a vibrancy and verve relevant to contemporary needs. It was a man who was put to death at 33 who transformed religion for all time.

A proper appreciation of youthful endeavour should not, however, decry the value of experience, especially in spiritual things. Those who most clearly sensed the significance and wonder of the birth of Jesus included the venerable Simeon and a 90-year-old prophet, Anna.

Pastoral responsibility has many rewards and one of them is the privilege of spending time with the aged saints whose bodies are failing greatly, but whose spirituality is deep and keen. That depth comes from long and intimate acquaintance with their Lord, often arising from the time for reflection that immobility brings. I have often experienced the depth of their inner vision. The most accurate comments I ever heard on the spiritual life of the congregation to which she was attached, came from a 90-year-old woman, confined to a wheelchair, living alone and for years unable to attend

20. 1997.

church. The 'closer walk with God' that the life of virtual solitude brings seems to strengthen the spiritual instinct and intuition of some people to a point where it can result in true prophecy.

Age, not always crabbed, and youth, given the gift of grace, can surely 'live together'. Each has something to offer the other. There is a tendency, at least in Western society, for age to be discounted, even disparaged, but it is a mistake not to be willing to listen to the wisdom that years bring. Quantity in years alone does not, however, necessarily bring about the evolution of spiritual quality. A very young man had to tell a senior citizen, the Pharisee Nicodemus, that 'you must be born again'. It was for that same young man to tell a much older fisherman: 'Get thee behind me, Satan, for thou savourest not the things that be of God but those that be of men'.

For young people to see visions and for older people to dream dreams, said Peter at Pentecost (quoting the prophet Joel), can be evidence of the outpouring of the Spirit. In the economy of the kingdom, inner vision in older and younger people together could be a powerful instrument for good.

Sustaining Grace

Corruption is much more contagious than holiness. That is why the struggle to develop a spirituality, be it corporate or personal, is such a demanding one. It is not easy to live 'life in the Spirit', to adhere to things that are 'good and lovely and of good report' in the materialistic, competitive, even ruthless world we experience today.

The opening statement above was prompted by a curious and controversial passage in one of the minor prophets of the Old Testament, the prophecies of Haggai. The passage is in chapter 2, verses 10–14. There is much difference of view among scholars as to its correct interpretation. Here, only the central point of the passage can be considered. The priests are asked for a directive on the infectiousness of holiness in a certain sacrificial context. It is not possible, they say, for one holy object to spread holiness to other objects. But when uncleanliness is involved, it is quite different. The contagiousness of uncleanliness is real. The detail of the directive is unimportant here, but the general principle thrown up by the question is disturbing. Is it our experience that it is, in fact, much easier for us to be corrupted than to be sanctified? It is depressing to realize that it is indeed so.

There is a long-established religious view that is much simpler for humanity to choose evil rather than good, darkness rather than light; to be more vulnerable to the attraction of conforming to this world than being spiritually transformed within it. Both biblical testimony to the subtlety of sin and psychology's awareness of the dark, negative inner pressures coming from the shadow side of the unconscious bear this out. If it is true that we are more vulnerable to negative pressures than positive ones, more liable to temptation than able to resist it, then there is much in contemporary life and attitudes that inflates our problem. To be affluent can make us more vulnerable to greed than to poverty. When money comes to be loved, and there is plenty of advertising to stimulate the desire for money, materialism can develop dangerously. Indeed, so weighted are the contrary factors that a sustained search for spirituality is a major task.

It would, however, be totally inconsistent with the religious spirit to lose heart or give up. It is of the very essence of the committed life to ask, seek, knock, search and struggle towards the light. And thanks are due to those outstanding people who, mostly unsung, encourage us on the spiritual way.

It is of the generosity of God that grace is given to those who are prepared to walk by faith: saving grace, sustaining grace, sanctifying grace. Those who use the means of grace that are provided – prayer, worship, sacraments, fellowship – will find that, on the road to a greater spirituality, we can make especial progress when we know that we are not alone.

The Dayspring

'The day sprynge or dawnynge of the days giveth a certeine lyght before the rysinge of the sonne', writes a sixteenth-century author speaking of the 'dayspring', a word used in the books of Job and St. Luke. That image became reality for my friend Jillian and I one late September morning.

Due to a meeting in north London in the evening, we had to leave the lovely, car-free island of Tresco in the Scillies at 6 a.m. It needed seven forms of transport to get us to the church on time! First, from the hotel, was the tractor-drawn trailer with its two bench-seats and a rail to grab, then a specially provided boat to ferry us to St. Mary's, the main island. An airport coach was waiting to take us to catch the first helicopter of the day to Penzance. From there a minibus to Penzance station, and then a five-hour train journey to London Paddington. Finally, a taxi took an hour to struggle through traffic to complete what should have been a half-hour run to north London, reminding us of the worst aspects of city life.

It was between Tresco and St. Mary's that dawn began to break over St. Martin's (another island in the Scillies), exactly as the writer of long ago described it. The experience was a moving, indeed thrilling one, as that 'certeine lyght' appeared just before sunrise. It spoke of a new day, a new beginning, and new opportunities, and it underlined an image strongly present in the gospels, where the coming of Christ is described as a light shining in the darkness. How beautifully Zechariah, the father of John the Baptist, spoke with prophetic insight of the coming of the Messiah. 'You will be the Lord's forerunner,' he said (as Luke reports in William Barclay's translation) 'to prepare the road which he will travel' and to tell of 'the deep compassion of our God which has graciously sent heaven's dawn to break upon us, to shine on those who sit in darkness and in the shadow of death, and to direct our steps in the roads that lead to peace'.

'The people that walked in darkness have seen a great light,' prophesied Isaiah. 'The light' continues to shine in the darkness, 'and the darkness has never extinguished it'. In that lies our hope.

'The heavenly Jerusalem is not in some dream of the future. It is now. One only needs to open one's eyes.' [21] That encouraging statement was made by a Indian holy man on his deathbed. Too often, the sheer weight of the world's evil overwhelms us, its materialism blinds us, and its pain and suffering desensitize us. Look then towards 'the dayspring from on high who has visited us', to sense the dawn with its 'certeine lyght,' to find around us so much that is good – marvellous gifts of creation, inspiration in the creative arts. Look at the multitude of good and loving people who, stimulated by their faith, whatever their religion, pour compassion into a needy world. Jerusalem, heaven, the Kingdom of God is now. We need to open our eyes, minds, hearts, souls, and gladly embrace it.

21. Quoted by Donald Nicholl in *Holiness*, Darton, Longman & Todd, 1996.

The Divine Jigsaw

You cannot argue with a man born blind when he says categorically: 'Whereas I was blind, now I see'. Personal experience, as the Pharisees, critical of Jesus, had to accept, was the proof of a miracle. The interpretation of the event is another matter. For the recipient of the miracle there is the logical conclusion: 'If this man were not of God, he could do nothing' and therefore the only possible reaction: 'Lord, I believe'. The Pharisees' not-so logical conclusion was that 'this man is not of God because he keepeth not the sabbath day'. But they did not have his *personal* experience.

Experience is the ultimate ground of conviction. Robert Llewellyn, widely known for his spiritual writing and particularly as Chaplain of the Julian Cell in Norwich from 1976 to 1990, testifies to the doctrine of providence through his personal experience. At the age of 89, with a huge span of hindsight, he can say: 'My life has been like a large jigsaw puzzle where it has often been impossible to see how this or that contributed to the picture, but as the whole has come together, the purpose has been made clear'. Many will respond to that testimony and be ready to bear witness to their personal experiences of divine providence and their conviction that 'all things work together for good to those who love God'.

Similarly, testimony will gladly be offered by those who, as a matter of personal experience, have known the extraordinary reach of divine forgiveness and the profound mystery of God's healing ways. But there is a difference between the personal experience with which we began and the convictions about providence, forgiveness and healing just expressed. At the heart of the first incident is one objective fact that neither recipient nor observer can deny. Eyes have been opened and a blind man can see. The latter experiences are not based on those sorts of facts but only on personal interpretations of events. In other words, in the first case there is an *objective* fact. In the second, apart from the possibility of a medical miracle of healing, conclusions are dependent on subjective factors. These may feel unquestionably reliable to the believer, but they are incapable of proof to the observer. Therein lies the problem of personal experience as a proof-text in matters of faith.

There is always the need for an objective standard by which to test convictions drawn from personal experience, and it is the great Reformation emphasis on the Word of God as the supreme rule of faith and life that supplies this.

Only by testing experience against the Word of God can we be confirmed in our wonder at the way God deals with us through divine forgiveness, providence and healing. That is the way to 'firm foundations'.

Why Me?

The best of texts can become clichés if used excessively, inappropriately or irrelevantly. That could even happen to such moving words as 'Well done, good and faithful servant. Enter into the joy of your Lord.' At the funeral service I had to conduct last week, I had no hesitation, however, in using those words to sum up the life of a relative who had died, full of years and with a magnificent record of service to the church, to people and good causes. Committed to her marriage and her family, to the members of the various organizations she served, to those allocated to her for pastoral care, she seemed, as much if not more than most, to deserve that 'Well done!' But alongside such a positive life, well worthy of the thanksgiving offered, there was a shadowed side, expressed in disappointments, losses and personal tragedies. She felt herself almost singled out for misfortune and she had every right to be bitter, for the family losses she suffered were enormous. But though never herself blaming God, she was entitled to ask 'Why me?'.

Much has been said of the 'curse of the Kennedys' following the deaths in an air crash of John F. Kennedy Jnr., his wife and sister-in-law. The inference has been made that there are individuals and families who seem to be chosen to suffer disproportionately in life. But the question 'Why us?' hovers in the background wherever those professing a religious faith suffer grievously.

'What I feared has come upon me', Job cried. 'What I dreaded has happened to me. I have no peace, no quietness, no rest, but only turmoil'. However, 'No one said a word to Job because they saw how great his suffering was'. The 'blameless and upright' Job was, according to the Old Testament story, being tested by God through a catalogue of disasters.

'All these things are against me.' Again the despairing

71

cry against 'outrageous fortune' comes from the heart of Jacob as he bewails the loss of his sons Simeon and Reuben and the impending loss of Benjamin.

The stories differ but the underlying question is the same. There is a mystery in suffering which is beyond our understanding. Is there nothing but a combination of circumstances in the appalling things that happen to people? Is there a purpose involved – with the divine role under scrutiny but beyond comprehension? Can a loving God be present when bad things happen to good people? 'Why me?'

The mystery remains. How the Kennedys cope with their tragic history, time will tell. Of Job, it is written that 'the Lord blessed the latter part [of his life] more than the first'. Jacob's feared losses would in due time lead to the dawning future of Israel. My relative's conjunction of triumphant discipleship and tragic experience combined to create a living faith and a life of service. Suffering remains a mystery which usually defies logic, but sometimes develops maturity. It is those who suffer most who sense that it can be a means of grace.

Sense of Purpose

One of the consequences of a bereavement, a broken relationship, or a redundancy notice is the death of a sense of purpose. The sadness of the widow, bereft of the partner of a lifetime, proclaims, not through word but through expression, that 'there is no point in going on'. 'A woman scorned' will, after the fury, feel the desperation of loneliness. Unemployment will lead to depression and despair, both through financial consequences and, even more, the loss of the dignity of work. The life that has lost its purpose and meaning can indeed become a desolate and derelict one.

The statistics of depression reflect such loss of purpose and meaning. It is an illness that is becoming one of the most prevalent of our time, nationally and internationally. It is not clinical or endogenous depression that incapacitates so many people – rather it is depression that is a reaction to circumstances. This is nevertheless real and, for many, devastating and debilitating. It follows serious disturbance of the equilibrium of life and is a response to changed and damaged physical circumstances (traumatic events brought about by war, natural disaster, famine, economic failure), emotional circumstances (bereavement, grief, loss, hurt, abuse, etc.), spiritual circumstances (the crisis of 'faith and doubt'). And it may be that the last is as serious as any other circumstance. As the 'ancient landmarks' of belief and creed are removed; as the fundamental tenets of inherited faith are questioned – not only by those hostile to religious faith, but from within the Church itself; as the traditional religious bases of ethics and behaviour are undermined, the 'deep roots and firm foundations' become destabilized.

Nihilism is an expression of that movement from faith and morality, showing itself in cynicism, boredom, lack of concern, emptiness, meaninglessness. The spiritual dangers inherent in such loss of purpose are very much expressed in the corporate depression threatening to encompass society.

Religious faith ought to be showing (through its preachers, and perhaps even more its pastors) that it is the realm in which purpose is nurtured and meaning developed; that the story of the Old Testament and the New is of people 'called' to a purpose within a faith that provides insights into ultimate meaning and truth. 'The life of faith is a continually renewed grasp of meaning in the midst of meaninglessness' wrote the late Lesslie Newbigin.

The sense of vocation, the conviction of being 'called', the feeling of being chosen to serve, lies deeply in the hearts of all who are convinced their life's purpose is in service. It is that sense of purpose which drives men and women on, overcoming obstacles, riding crises, undeterred and undefeated.

'But what if I fail of my purpose here?' writes Robert Browning. 'It is but to keep my nerves at strain, to dry one's eyes and laugh at a fall, and baffled, get up and begin again.' Or in historic words: 'To fight and fight and fight again'.

A sense of purpose provides the ability to go on.

Life's Music

Whether it is the conducting of an orchestra, the managing of a football team or the leading of a congregation, it is the skill and ability of the leader, in bringing the best out of each individual involved, which leads to success. Those who carry such roles have a great responsibility but they also enjoy a sense of satisfaction and fulfilment. In dealing with individuals, the teaching profession, in particular, remains a vocation – in that it offers the opportunity to 'educate' young people, that is (by derivation) to 'bring out' the potential gifts and talents of each girl or boy, stimulating a developing human being, mentally, physically, emotionally and indeed spiritually. Whatever impedes that process – socially, politically or economically – must be a matter of concern.

Such an ability characterized the way in which Jesus dealt with individual people. Whether choosing disciples or encountering people in need, his capacity for hearing a cry for help, ministering to a need and touching a nerve led the apostle, John, to comment that 'Jesus knew what was in man'. People grew taller in his presence, whether it was an extrovert, outspoken fisherman or his introvert brother; an anxious Pharisee seeking spiritual help or a Samaritan woman at a well; a ruler of the synagogue pleading for his dying daughter, or a Syro-Phoenician woman expressing a level of faith beyond his expectation. Jesus sensed, drew out and developed the strength and potential of those he encountered in his ministry. Indeed, nothing is more dramatic than the extraordinary change that compelled his scattered followers to seek to 'conquer the world' in his name. The transformation was brought about by that 'other Comforter', Pentecost's proof of Jesus's continuing presence and power.

There is in Christianity a proper emphasis on sin as a

negative factor, conditioning all we are and do. Consciousness of sin properly forms part of each act of worship in prayers of confession. But respect for, and belief in, the corrupting effect of (as Genesis presents it) 'disobedience to the divine will', should never blind us to the wonder of creation and the reality of human potential. A dramatic reminder of that comes in the words of Jolan Chang – words that compel us to ask questions about our achievements, especially when seen within the context of a faith which makes weakness strong, turns darkness into light, and speaks of death and resurrection: 'Most of us are like owners of a precious Stradivarius violin that we have never learned to play'. What a gift of creation is human 'be-ing'! What potential the Creator has implanted in stamping us with the divine image! What grounds for hope and encouragement lie there! Life is more than 'being'. It is 'becoming'.

Those outside a religious faith may hear this challenge to 'learn to play' as a call to positive thinking, renewed endeavour, and recovery of energy and purpose. For those who acknowledge a divine power, it is a reminder that it is never too late to take further lessons in how to create life's lovelier music.

Missed Opportunity

In pastoral ministry, it can happen that a need is expressed and a response is not offered. Subsequent sorrow and remorse inevitably follow. It may be that a visit is required, but for reasons of pressure, time or commitments, it is not made. Or it may be that a letter needs to be sent, but it never gets written.

A letter is a pastoral tool of great importance. Paul used it to notable effect, to expound his theology to the various churches he had founded, but also (as the latter part of most of his letters demonstrate) to convey pastoral concern about people. Down through literary history, the letter has been a means of making needs known and meeting them, expressing feelings that could not be spoken, giving and receiving love and compassion, strengthening and encouraging someone in distress. The prompting of the inner spirit to 'write' needs to be heeded too, because failure to respond to it may create a missed opportunity.

It is a failure in that latter field that is the reason for encouraging others to write when the spirit moves them. For it may be, in a real sense, a call to a ministry which is pastoral at heart.

For me, there was a disturbing moment of truth came when I was shown a newspaper tribute to Professor Iain Dea, the distinguished scientist who specialised in polysaccharide chemistry. Scientists all over the world paid tribute to his work and the benefits it has brought to people. His death announced a missed opportunity on my part.

I had not seen Iain in 45 years, since he had been in my Sunday School in Juniper Green, Edinburgh, and a playmate of our children, but I remember his parents well. They both died in 1996, one in January and the other in July. Between his mother's and his father's death, both his parents-in-law died. At Christmas time that same year Iain became ill. In the following three years Iain's cancer developed and became terminal.

I mention this sequence not because it is a further graphic example of the mystery of suffering, but because I regret so much the missed opportunity I was given when I met Iain's aunt soon after his parents' deaths. She asked me to re-establish contact with Iain and in some way to minister to him in his bereavements. At the height of his career, happily married and in mid-life, there seemed to be time to develop the connection. In the mass of correspondence, the piles and files of papers so typical of studies, church offices and even many a home, that necessary letter was never given the pastoral priority it deserved.

The experience underlines the importance of the written word in the personal, pastoral ministry which everyone can offer. It emphasizes the need to catch the sound of, and listen to, the voice within, as messages from the unconscious seek to bring the urgent priority of meeting some personal need to our conscious notice. Sensitivity to need involves sensitivity to time and the organization of our priorities not in terms of choice, but of commitment.

III. Church and Community

A Time To Die

'There is a time to die', wrote the Preacher (Ecclesiastes) in the Old Testament. It is a truth on which organizations, not least religious ones, should sometimes reflect. Too often, when these bodies – much respected and greatly loved – are moving into decline, they redouble their efforts to continue their existence. Those who fight hardest to 'keep going' are usually older people who, having seen and known the benefits of belonging to a group with a particular purpose, believe new generations should receive similar blessings from it.

The reality is different. Times move on. Needs change. What one generation feels is essential may have little or no relevance to another generation. The trouble is that when the members of an organization feel the need to keep the group alive, all the available energy is drawn into maintaining the organization while leaving too little time or thought for the aims and purposes for which the body was originally created. Perspective and priorities become victims of the overriding desire to continue 'at all costs'. It should sometimes be recognized that there is a time to die and that, paradoxically, death, if accepted gracefully, can lead to the possibility of new life.

One respected organization in the field of health and healing has faced this issue and is hoping that its resulting course of action will open the door to new life and positive gain in the field it has served for 54 years. The interdenominational, interdisciplinary Churches' Council for Health and Healing died on 31 December 1999. Founded by William Temple to promote co-operation between medicine and religion, it sought to fulfil that purpose by bringing together all the mainstream denominations, the healing organizations, the Royal Colleges of Medicine and related disciplines. To fulfil this co-ordinating role, a structure evolved over the years to meet the responsibilities the Council had in relation to health and healing. The sheer weight and complexity of that increasingly irrelevant structure was one of the core factors in persuading those responsible for its work to decide to recommend closure.

But there is dramatic irony in this situation! The field of health and healing is one of the growth points in the life of the Church. More churches than ever are holding regular healing services. A major report on health and healing will be presented to the Anglican Church by its working party in the near future.* Meetings have recently taken place between senior clergy and doctors to encourage co-operation in the area of health and wholeness. The Churches' Council for Health and Healing has fulfilled its brief by making such developments possible.

When a purpose is accomplished, the time to die may have arrived. But in its freeing of energy and resources, human and financial, it will be a death that leads to life. That theme of death and resurrection belongs to essential Christianity.

* Published in the spring of 2000 by Church House, London S.W. 1.

To Do Justly

Widespread corruption, lust for power, rampant idolatry and political arrogance that finds no place for God – is this a comment on our times? In fact it is a prophet's analysis of the profound faults he saw in his nation's life long ago. The prophet Micah had much to say to Judah about social injustice, sleaze and public hypocrisy. He also criticized the formality of ritual sacrifice. 'Shall I come before him with burnt offerings . . . with thousands of rams . . . with ten thousand rivers of oil?' asks Micah with the irony of hyperbole, but it leads to a great statement about the true nature of personal, and indeed corporate, religion. What does the Lord really require? It is justice and fairness, mercy and compassion, humility and respect for God.

It would be insensitive to plead for personal commitment to justice and fairness. We are all surely committed to 'doing justly'. But in the public world, there are constant cries of 'It's not fair!' Many very unhappy people are complaining fervently against present disability legislation and unfair cuts. Senior citizens' organizations are doing the same over pensions, and there is much unease in some communities over the unjust ways in which different groups are treated.

The call to social righteousness in a world created by a God who (Jesus tells us) values each individual is always before the Church. Society must not only seek to do justly – but must be seen to do it.

The personal call to 'love mercy' can again be taken as agreed. We may not always achieve it, but the standard is clear, for compassion is integral to religion. The corporate call to mercy is more complicated. Can the state do justly *and* love mercy? Wherever the concept of mercy is related to justice, controversy is inevitable, as is seen in high-profile issues that have divided society and caused major problems for the politicians who have to deal with them. This country is, however, widely seen as compassionate; it is a reputation not to be discarded lightly. And whatever further problems remain over debt, the cancellation of so-called Third World dues by this country in response to pressure from the public and the Church, is an act of corporate mercy that is to the credit of this nation.

The call to 'walk humbly with God' is certainly made to individuals, and each one of us constantly needs to hear it. Living life without God comes too easily because of the pressures of contemporary materialism and secularism. Corporately, the public arrogance in dispensing with any acknowledgement of and respect for God, which so troubled Micah, is all too clearly a mark of our time.

The prophets saw clearly what would happen as a result of living without any sense of the spiritual. It would be national disaster. The reminder to do justly and to love mercy, and the exhortation to walk humbly with God, is relevant prophecy today.

True Compassion

The most plaintive question asked in the Old Testament is surely that in the Lamentations of Jeremiah. Reflecting on the destruction, desolation and despair in Jerusalem, Jeremiah cries out: 'It is nothing to you, all ye that pass by?' In other words, does anybody care?

The sermon I heard at a famous Glasgow church did not make any great impression at the time, but looking back over some forty years I realize its central message did register. It was a simple one, but an important one. Commenting on Jesus's visit to the house where Peter's mother-in-law had taken ill, the preacher (Dr Ernest Jarvis of Wellington Church) was at pains to stress the sensitivity of Jesus. He did not only see her there. He did something more, he 'took notice' of her and acted to heal her. It is a factor that is equally important in caring relationships, professional or personal. It is imperative that those who care do not simply listen to words that are used, but 'hear' what is being said. It is the point made in Stevie Smith's poem: 'He's not waving, but drowning'.

The same question might have been asked as Jesus hung from the cross on Calvary. For some it was a very distressing experience. But to others it was nothing, a familiar sight where crucifixion was a public punishment. Like Pilate, passers-by could wash their hands of it.

The question might well be asked of us all in times of great suffering. Do we only see it – but fail to take notice of it? Do we listen to – but fail to hear – the cries that come from those in despair? Are we actually moved to compassion? To action?

It is right to recognize what we cannot do. But there still remains the call, especially in painful personal situations, to reach a level of sensitivity greater than that we normally show as part of our attempt to 'try always to have the same attitude to life as Jesus had' [22].

If, in our attitude to others' need, we seek to express the mind of Christ, we must have a compassionate heart, an active mind, sensitive intuition, a dedicated imagination, a disciplined will and a soul with sincere desire. Then we will take note of needs, hear desperate cries and find physical strength to respond as far as we can.

Our capacity to serve is confined by the limitations we have, both physical and emotional, but these have often been shown to be capable of expansion through 'the grace which is sufficient'. 'She has done what she could', said Jesus of the woman who had washed his feet with her tears and dried them with her hair. To make whatever effort we can carries the approval of the Lord.

22. Philippians 2:5 (William Barclay's translation).

Gratitude and Hope

The world is saturated with words: millions of them appear each day in books, magazines, journals, learned papers, and newspapers that grow bigger and bigger to encompass every aspect of life in numerous 'sections' and colour magazines.

The same is true in the religious field. In the trade journal that deals with bookselling, the 'religious' category is one of the biggest. Whether it is inspirational anecdotes or heavy theology, many millions of words are offered to us to shape and guide our thinking. Is it all necessary to cope with life and its needs? Are intellectuals better at handling life's problems than, as the New Testament would describe them, 'the common people' who (we are told) 'heard Jesus gladly'? He gave them not the theological minutiae so valued by the official teachers of religion in his time, but the truth in a form they could understand.

Professor Noam Chomsky, in a recent BBC Radio 3 interview, described the three revolutions that have changed the world as: the computer revolution and the microchip, the genetic code, and the fundamental change in the way we understand the mind and language. But for many, especially of an older generation, the computer remains a mystery beyond understanding, while discussions about genetics can be too technical for most people. Being illiterate in computers and trying hard to understand genetic mysteries, I had to struggle too to comprehend Professor Chomsky and his broadcast! It is easy to feel decidedly deficient in one's ability to cope with the complexities of the contemporary world!

Of course we need to study philosophy, psychology, sociology and theology if we are to understand and deal with the issues of our time – and especially to preach about them – but sometimes the very simplicity of statements from, for example, aged saints or profoundly spiritual writers with a capacity for turning profundity into simplicity, take us further along the road to coping with life and its problems.

Jillian and I visited a lady in her nineties recently. She gave herself 'one out of ten' for her physical state, but she deserves a very much higher rating for her mental ability and memory. She is widely read and very much in touch with world affairs, but lives her life now in terms of a philosophy summed up in a simple phrase, passed on to her by an archbishop friend quoting a lady whom he had met. 'I goes to bed thankful, and I wakes up hopeful', she told him. Gratitude and hope are essential to a happy life.

We need the academic, the intellectual, the philosopher, the sage and the scholar with their contributions to the world's thinking. Long may they make them! But how welcome too is the simplicity of the saints who, with gratitude and hope, live their lives 'in the hands of God'. To meet such people is a blessing indeed. They bear witness to their faith – without any words.

When Words Fail

Words fail us. There are none that can describe our feelings following the IRA bomb in Omagh [23]. In the presence of shattered bodies, shattered lives, shattered minds, shattered faith, words seem totally irrelevant. What can be said in the face of such evil, such grief, such pain? And so Omagh is added to the agonising roll-call of places which will be forever associated with death, destruction and despair – and it feels in such a short period of time – Bradford, Hillsborough, Lockerbie, Zeebrugge, King's Cross, *The Marchioness*, Dunblane. How can human beings blow other human beings out of the sky? Fire randomly at innocent schoolchildren? Destroy, in the most callous and cruel way, the children, the parents, the people of Omagh? Words fail us . . .

History is strewn with unspeakable situations: the hell of the Holocaust, the horror of Hiroshima. They are there too in the Bible – the slaughter of the innocents at the command of King Herod, the distress of King David and his men after finding their wives and daughters taken captive at Ziklag.

There will never be a time when life will 'get back to normal' in Omagh, nor can families bereaved by such a monstrous evil event be expected to cope with that experience. Yet somehow living goes on . . . as it has done after the murder of the schoolchildren in Dunblane. It is only those in the very midst of the suffering who will learn how to do this. It will come not through theory, but of necessity. For some the resources will lie within their families, through the bond of shared pain; others will find them with friends and neighbours, themselves victims of the blast, or shocked spectators of it; some will find it in the fellowship of their church or club or community activity. Some will find it in compassion from friends and strangers. Some may find it in their faith.

23. The bomb planted in Omagh in August 1998.

But it will not be in theories about suffering. It will be in the knowledge that the Jesus who wept over the death of a friend and over the desolation of Jerusalem, is the one who himself suffered at the hands of wicked people, who endured agony in Gethsemane and cruelty on Calvary, who was despised and rejected, who was acquainted with grief.

There is no answer to the problem of suffering, nor any explanation as to how human beings can be capable of the cruelty that crucified Omagh. There will, however, in due course, come from the people in that community some witness to their belief that, in the darkest hour of their lives, the suffering God was there with them, not to explain the inexplicable, but to weep with them in their desolation. As it was said at Dunblane, the first tears would be God's tears.

Careful Words

The evidence for the presence of reporters following Jesus during his ministry, it has been said jocularly, is the third verse of St. Luke's Gospel, in the Authorised Version. Zacchaeus, anxious to see Jesus but being a little man, 'could not [see him] for the press'. This somewhat archaic way of referring to crowd problems has nothing, of course, to do with journalists, but it may serve to introduce a discussion of the responsibilities of those who work with words.

The issue is a relevant one, especially as we approach the anniversary of the death of Diana, Princess of Wales. There is an art in remembering, which must be nourished as the time of remembrance comes, but it really does involve care with words.

Oliver Tomkins, formerly the Bishop of Bristol, has written a very searching prayer, in his book *Asking God* [24]. It is relevant to those who work with words: 'O God, deliver us from the abstract words that hide men and women behind a cloud; deliver us from the untrue words that value sensation more than the facts; deliver us from the emotive words that rouse our feelings at the expense of our minds; and guard, through the Word himself, all those who follow the dangerous trade of dealing in words'. These are wise words indeed.

When St. Paul wrote (in his Hymn of Love, I Corinthians 13) that 'love rejoiceth not in iniquity but rejoiceth in the truth', he touched a nerve relating to human weakness. William Barclay, in his translation of the same passage, makes the thrust of that statement even stronger. He puts it: 'Love finds nothing to be glad about when things go wrong, but is glad when truth is glad'. That statement, of course, describes the ideal more than actuality, for there is some-

24. *Asking God*, by Oliver Tomkins, Darton, Longman & Todd.

90

thing in human nature – it is surely part of our fallen nature – that is (to put it at its best) interested in the things that go wrong for others. The media is therefore often accused of publishing mainly bad news. And as newspapers need high sales, and radio and television require good listening and viewing figures, one can only conclude that the media is providing what the public wants, namely sensation. Gossip is a human weakness. Circulation is built on the suffering of others. Hopefully, we fall short of being glad when someone goes wrong, but we are, alas, all too interested in such events.

'Take with you words . . . take away all iniquity; accept that which is good and we will render the fruit of our lips' – and pens, computers and the internet. The words of Hosea are taken out of context, but they underline, for each one of us, our responsibility for what we say, write, broadcast, publish or read. If it is true that 'to every thing there is a time and a season', now is a time for particular care with words.

The Silence of the Tongue

'Careless talk costs lives'. Those who remember the Second World War will recall the poster campaign to compel people to think before they spoke, lest they carelessly conveyed information that might help the enemy. Careless talk has, this week, done a great deal of damage, causing bitter hurt to people with disabilities [25], provoking a monumental row that, even though it was in the context of sport, involved government ministers, even the Prime Minister. It has blighted a brilliant professional career. 'It's very easy to talk', said Mrs Mantalini in Dickens' *Nicholas Nickleby*, but if you 'chance to talk a little wild' as Henry VIII (in Shakespeare's play of that name) commented and do it as a so-called celebrity in a media-conscious age, the consequences can be, and often are, serious.

The reading at our ministry of healing service on Sunday – from St. James's letter in the New Testament – happened to be on the theme of what Mother Teresa calls 'the silence of the tongue'. This is surely the most down-to-earth letter among the epistles in the New Testament. James does not soar to theological heights as Paul did in the intricacies of his letter to the Romans. But he is extremely practical. He hates sham ('Faith without works is dead'). It is James who has most to say about the power for good and evil of the tongue. 'What a huge forest fire can be set ablaze by the tiniest spark', he writes, underlining its inherent power.

Mother Teresa's similar emphasis on the importance of the silence of the tongue re-echoes James's point, which is the need to recognize that the tongue can be both 'an unruly evil' or the medium through which we praise God. The choice is ours! We can (Mother Teresa says) 'refrain from every word that causes darkness, turmoil, and death'.

---

25. The reference is to the England football manager, Glenn Hoddle, who lost his position as a result of a remark that related disability to punishment.

We must use it for 'praising God and speaking the life-giving word of truth, that is the truth which enlightens and inspires, brings peace, hope and joy'.

It is almost 2000 years since James spoke with fervour about careless talk. It is within our times that Mother Teresa has encouraged the silence of the tongue. Both James and Mother Teresa need to be heard today. It has been shown how a careless, thoughtless statement can hurt and offend people with disabilities, and a heavy price was paid for this obvious error. But the subtler ways in which we all talk carelessly about people with disability also create pain and grief. Terms such as 'the handicapped', 'people of that kind' or 'invalids' demonstrate the lack of awareness and sensitivity which hurts so much.

It is important to speak the truth, but it must be done in love. It is that qualification which will help us to avoid the careless talk that so damages lives.

The Centre-man

Early in 1918, seven months before the end of the First World War, twelve men of the 2/1 Wessex Field Ambulance Unit asked the padre, appropriately named Donald Standfast, to form an association for various small groups meeting under his leadership at the Soldiers' Club in Bethune, France, a base behind the front line. 'Our essential idea is to form a fellowship in which we may assist each other to live the Christian life', they said. They often met under fire. 'Living or dying', they felt fellowship with Christ to be their greatest need. Standfast intended this 'league of fellowship' to close down at the Armistice. It didn't. Appeals led him, in March 1919, to make it into the Regnal League in Rouen. In 1999, it was 80 years old.

I thought my experience in ecumenical organizations and interdenominational journalism had made me aware of all the national bodies whose purpose, like the Regnal League, is to explore wholeness of life. I have to confess that up to a month or two ago, I had never heard of the Regnal League. It does not seem to have made an effective public impact. Having addressed Regnal's 69th annual conference and learned of their existence and history, I feel that it is a great pity that the movement is not better known. It has something to offer.

Its vow is worth recording. The Commitments of Membership involve 'the endeavour to be a true friend to all, not allowing myself by word or deed to do injury to anyone, to take care of my body and seek to develop my mental gifts for the sake of others. With the help of God, I will seek Wholeness of Life.' It is not narrow in outlook but encourages tolerance, openness and sharing in friendship. It is earthed in the real world in that it is committed to seek wholeness for society too. Its belief is not in rule, but in love. 'A rule can never be enough for a Christian.

It has to be a love springing from the individual heart towards God.'

The quest for wholeness, health, healing, maturity, individuation, eternal life, whichever term is your particular choice, is in effect the journey of life. The achievement of it, in Christian terms, is dependent on the gift of grace and the energy of the Holy Spirit. The process is not, however, a purely personal one. Changed people change situations. The Incarnation compels active involvement in the health and healing of society, too.

I am glad to have come upon the Regnal League. Broad-based, open, non-directive, non-judgemental, creative, it is not a substitute for the Church, but is a bridge to it. Its local groups are, appropriately given their emphasis on wholeness, 'circles'. The focus throughout the Regnal League is on the One who 'reigns', that is Christ. Indeed they have a name for Jesus which sums up their faith. They say he is 'the Centre-man'.

Need for Grace

One of the most entertaining obituaries I have ever seen appeared in the *Daily Telegraph* last week. I enjoyed it immensely. That seems surprising, for death is not a subject for enjoyment or entertainment. It is a time for sadness. It brings hurt and pain, and tears. But it is this relationship between sadness and laughter which makes the obituary of Ambrose Appelbe noteworthy.

Ambrose was 95 when he died, 'an inveterate founder of causes, some worthy, some eccentric'. The 'worthy' ones included his part in the creation of the National Marriage Guidance Council and War on Want; the eccentric, the Smell Society (which he founded in concert with George Bernard Shaw and H. G. Wells). It sought to eliminate foul odours from society!

It was in 'worthy' causes that I met Ambrose when, as our solicitor, he was involved in the setting up of Highgate Counselling Centre in London, and later Westminster Pastoral Foundation. His generosity towards other causes in which I was involved was memorable.

Ambrose too would have read his obituary with a smile – the apparent contradictions in his life, the ironies, the delightful hint of the eccentric. The son of a Methodist minister, Ambrose, in his professional work as a solicitor, defended Mandy Rice-Davies (in the Christine Keeler case in the sixties). His clients included Ingrid Bergman and the murderer John Christie. He defended Bertrand Russell as a conscientious objector and, with John Profumo at Toynbee Hall, worried about poverty and need. He admired Gandhi and tried to reflect his simple life. He worked for women's rights and childcare support, housing, bereavement and counselling. He admired concise prose and wrote legal letters in longhand. A co-founder of the Anatomical Donors

Association, his great age ironically prevented his own body being used for research! And there is so much more!

The paradoxical relationship between laughter and tears, joy and pain, acceptability and rejection (Ambrose experienced both) has a link with Palm Sunday. How contradictory were Jesus's welcome to Jerusalem and the institutionalised rejection he suffered there. 'Hosanna', they cried. 'Crucify him', they cried.

Abuse of power is a current theme, both in European and national contexts. People in high places have a daunting responsibility for it is through the use, or abuse, of power that the destinies of people and nations are determined. The crucifixion is a story of power abused; ecclesiastical power by the chief priests and elders, temporal power by two rulers who, through their mutual abrogation of responsibility, became friends.

Jesus alone could make and sustain the claim that 'all power' was given to him 'in heaven and on earth', for divine grace was his. If the events of Holy Week demonstrated the absence of grace in priests, rulers and the people of Jerusalem so long ago, may their memory bring back some grace to the world today. Society, and those in it who wield power, need it.

Unhealthy Sign

It is with real affection that I remember the village doctor in my first parish many, many years ago. A highly respected member of the community, he was indeed the archetypal family doctor. He was always available in times of need. When our infant son was dangerously ill, he was there. When our daughter was knocked down on the busy road outside our manse, it was not an unfamiliar member of a health centre team or an anonymous locum who happened to be on duty, who turned up. It was the doctor himself.

The doctor was my senior by more than 40 years. Perhaps it was that fact and some immaturity or inexperience I had shown that led him to offer me a gentle homily on the theme of responsibility.

The doctor enjoyed his 'dram' but always in his own home. He had, he told me, deliberately decided that however much he would have enjoyed socializing at the village inn, he would never drink there. The sight of him entering or leaving the public house might prove unhelpful to a 'weaker brother' – or sister – among his patients. I admired his sense of responsibility.

Such a sense of overriding public duty has, sadly, been missing in the unhappy saga presently being played out across the Atlantic. Personal desires and needs have not been made properly subservient to public responsibility [26]. It is a significant omission. Benjamin Zander, the internationally renowned conductor, when leading a master-class in London recently, said to us with emphasis: 'Never ask what's wrong; always ask what's missing.' In other words, avoid the futility of concentrating on purely negative elements in any situation. Rather, contribute the positive missing elements.

26. A reference to President Clinton's personal problems, 1998.

If a satisfactory sense of responsibility is one factor too often missing today, another is a sense of reverence. In a depressingly materialistic world, reverence, with its components wonder, awe and respect, has become a casualty of our times. Widespread vandalism and destruction show a lack of respect for property, while old age and the wisdom it implies are dismissed as irrelevant. A total lack of respect for human life and fellow human beings is expressed in violence, terrorism, murder, mugging, rape and abuse. Any residual respect for the sacred intimacies of personal relationships has disappeared, as every aspect of sexual behaviour, normal and abnormal, is openly paraded and, through modern technology, publicized internationally. Inevitably, a similar disrespect is extended to the sacred and the holy. No sense of the numinous (the divine) can remain as minor satirists and comedians rubbish God and all things spiritual. A society that is losing all sense of reverence is an unhealthy society.

Tennyson offers a challenge not only to the world, but to the churches, when he asks that 'more of reverence may dwell among us'. To recover the sense of holy awe and wonder so important to prophets, priests and people of old, may do something to redeem a world which idolizes wealth, glorifies the trivial and glamorizes sin.

Pastoral Dilemma

When I read commentators who say, as William Barclay does, that 'the best and most ancient (New Testament) manuscripts do not contain this story', I feel profoundly disappointed. In it Jesus speaks with authority on one of the great dilemmas of today. How should religious people make judgements about the behaviour of others? Priests and pastors constantly face this problem. Is it their responsibility to condemn – on biblical, theological or ethical grounds – certain behaviour within personal relationships, or should they consider the issues in terms of 'situation ethics'? The latter is, as David Edwards has written, 'making a judgement that the right solution to any moral problem depends much more on the situation itself than on any moral code'. And, he adds, 'the key to the solution is always love'. Contemporary attitudes are so often expressed either as sharply defined negative judgements, or else in terms of Alan Richardson's definition: 'The rightness of an action is to be judged in relation to the situation in which it takes place, rather than with reference to laws or universally binding rules.'

Issues at the heart of this tension include marriage, divorce, homosexuality, relationship situations of a triangular kind, living together, etc. Good people who feel bound by law can go through agony when they feel blessed by a love that is officially unacceptable. Pastors too can feel the pain of those who face them, struggling with the hurt of loving too much but bound by rules.

The story to which I referred is, of course, that of the adulterous woman in John's Gospel (8:1–11) It has such an authentic 'ring of truth' about Jesus that, as some commentators allow, it surely has (despite the technical textual difficulties) some foundation in fact.

The importance of the story lies in its demonstration of

Jesus's attitude to human problems. Firstly, he rightly denounces, in the most subtle of ways, the judgementalism that forgets that 'all have sinned', and that no one is qualified by their own righteousness to condemn others. Secondly, he acts out the great statement that God 'did not send his Son into the world to condemn the world but that the world through him might be saved'. 'Neither do I condemn you', he tells the woman. Thirdly, he says 'Go now and leave your life of sin behind.' That phrase is the answer to those who fear he has opened the door to moral licence and ethical irresponsibility.

Combining the need to give spiritual direction, with the obligation to love and accept the sinner while hating the sin, can create a traumatic tension for all who deal with personal problems. Always in the pastoral heart must be the awareness that 'there but for the grace of God, go I'.

Whether, as some specialists suggest, the story is technically dubious, or authentic as I sincerely feel, it is one that we should carry in both heart and mind when we attempt to deal creatively with human failure.

Sharing the Pain

Those who seek to care for others pastorally must have the ability not only to sympathize with them, but also to empathize with them, that is to understand their situation and to share their pain. This is especially so in times of loss and bereavement. To go on to identify with them may, however, be going a step too far. Every grief is unique, and no one else can fully enter into that suffering.

The danger of over-identification or being, as it were, taken over by others' problems, is a matter for constant attention in the supervision of counsellors and care professionals. That danger acknowledged, there is, however, the need to do everything possible to (as the Old Testament prophet Ezekiel put it) 'sit where they sit'. To identify as closely as possible with others' pain is to demonstrate a true empathy.

I found it necessary to recognize the important distinctions made above in talking recently to just under 200 bereaved parents. Every one had lost a child (or children) of various ages, and in various circumstances, and many of them had been recently bereaved. I spoke on 'Healing relationships: growth through friendship', a concept at the heart of the national and international organization of which very sadly (for membership means your child has died) they are members, The Compassionate Friends.* Being the only person there who was not a bereaved parent laid a heavy responsibility on me over every word I used. In particular, it would have been very insensitive to say 'I know how you feel.' I can't, for I have not been in their position.

That I was very nearly a bereaved parent is not relevant. Our son, when a few days old, contracted cellulitis and was saved by an experimental use (so far as very young babies were concerned) of the then new discovery of penicillin. He was brought back from near death. Nor does my lifelong vocational involvement, or my personal experience of bereavements, allow me to say to those who have suffered the greatest loss of all, the death of their son or daughter, 'I know how you feel.' What it does allow me to say, in empathy, is 'I feel for you.'

If ever sensitivity is needed, it surely is in times of bereavement. You cannot tell bereaved parents that 'time is a great healer, and you will get back to normal'. Whatever that normality was, it is gone for ever. You cannot assure people that they will 'get over it'. They never will. You cannot even assume that parents will 'come to terms with it'; most never do. You can only speak and act in such a way that, in that blackest hour and the long, dark days that follow it, you feel for them and with sensitive empathy try to say or do something that will comfort, encourage, sustain them; in other words, to offer a healing relationship.

* See note to Meditation Number 7.

Creative Irresponsibility

'Start a huge, foolish project like Noah,' wrote the thirteenth-century Persian poet, Rumi, 'it makes absolutely no difference what the world thinks of you.' I was indeed delighted to come across these words, for they expound a theme dear to my heart, that of creative irresponsibility.

Long-standing readers of these Meditations will recognize the phrase. 'Creative irresponsibility,' I wrote in 1994, 'springs from the sense of adventure which lies between prosaic responsibility and indefensible irresponsibility.' I pointed to an example of it in Abraham who, in obedience to his God, 'went out not knowing whither he went', taking risks with his family in the interests of a great cause. I recalled Paul's demand that we must be 'fools for Christ's sake' willing to be a public spectacle, insulted, persecuted, starving, for the sake of our convictions. 'Giving without counting the cost' can be creative indeed even if it is, in worldly terms, irresponsible.

Two examples of such risk-taking compel further reflection on this great concept and the need to re-emphasize it.

The first refers to a project called 'The Icebreaker Mission' and was recalled last year when its leading adventurer, Professor Jack Perry, died. That mission was undertaken by a group of businessmen – sixteen of them – who travelled to Peking in 1953 to establish trade agreements with China, shortly after the People's Republic of China had been proclaimed. The cold war made contact with China almost impossible. It was widely believed that the People's Republic would collapse, but Perry, a profound political thinker and prophet, took the opposite view. The stance made him unpopular in high places, unacceptable in official quarters, and the subject of criticism and opposition which endangered his business and his career. What can be achieved in and with China today remains unclear, but that which many saw as irresponsibility on Perry's part has done much to create opportunities for Sino-British relations in many spheres today.

The other example – and it was in this context that I quoted Rumi above – was the sheer irresponsibility of reconstructing Shakespeare's Globe Theatre on the banks of the Thames. The late Sam Wanamaker, the American actor who dreamed dreams and saw visions, started what many saw as 'a huge, foolish project' and, though he was not to see its completion, he inspired many others to press forward that endeavour. It is a moving example of creative irresponsibility.

Age dims the radicalism of youth, just as it can discourage risk and adventure, spiritually and mentally. But a living faith involves risk; theological risk in the endeavour to find relevant images and meaningful metaphors for contemporary seekers; ecumenical risk in the pursuit, not of uniformity, but unity; pastoral risk in seeking to minister to the relationships of the modern world. Launching out into the deep may sometimes be considered to be irresponsible. If it is a risk taken in obedience to the will of God, it will almost certainly have profoundly creative consequences, for active religion involves risk.

* See note to Meditation number 7.

The Unity of Light

It was cold indeed that night, with a biting, chilly wind that spoke of the depths of winter. It was very dark too for the hundreds of people gathered in the grounds of our local hospice. [27] But there was expectation also. In as long as it takes to press a switch, and in one movement, hundreds of bulbs on the huge horse chestnut tree in the grounds of the hospice would burst into light to proclaim the need to 'light up a life'.

'God is light and in him is no darkness at all', proclaimed one voice in the darkness. 'Light represents the attributes of God', said another. A third added: 'Physical light is but a true reflection of the true light in the world of reality, and that true light is God.' 'Then God said: "Let there be light" and there was light', added a fourth. But from whom and where did these four statements come? The last one was spoken by a Jewish rabbi, quoting the Old Testament. The first came from the Gospel of St. John and the Christian tradition. The second is an Upanishads message and was conveyed by a Hindu. The third was offered by a Muslim, quoting the Qur'an. That such differing traditions could unite to declare that God is light was a moving symbol of a unity which is compulsory in matters of life and death. In that the hospice offers a multi-faith approach to care, and acknowledges too that patients may have no religious faith or belief at all, the sole concern was to unite everyone from wherever they came in 'lighting up a life'.

Some caring organizations specifically and deliberately operate on a non-religious basis (The Compassionate Friends, in the field of bereavement, for example).* Such organizations are able to create unity in caring at a highly practical level, while acknowledging the right of members to

---

27. The North London Hospice, 47 Woodside Avenue, London N12 8TF.

have, or not to have, religious beliefs. It is an exercise in tolerance that – far from being criticized, as it sometimes is within the churches – deserves commendation. To allow religious rights to others does not in any way diminish one's own beliefs and convictions, nor does it prevent anyone from bearing witness to the things in which they most surely believe. To listen and learn need never be interpreted as a sign of weakness. Only by such attitudes can an understanding of others' views become possible. Only with understanding can that which is wrong be refuted. It is precisely those who stand on solid ground in their own beliefs who can most safely seek to understand and assess other approaches to faith.

Jesus, as Luke records, saw his ministry in terms of preaching, healing and liberty. Freedom in Christ is positive and energizing. It is not licence. There is no New Testament warrant for behaviour with no bounds, or belief with no boundaries. True freedom is a mature and living faith, which can engage confidently with a hostile world.

* See note to Meditation number 7

The Art of Remembering

Fifty-three memorial works were sensitively distributed among the trees, lawns, gardens and grounds of Blickling Hall near Aylsham in Norfolk, for an eight-month exhibition entitled The Art of Remembering. It provided a memorable and moving experience.

Its purpose was not related directly to the anniversary in August [28] of the deaths of Diana, Princess of Wales and of Mother Teresa, but its theme cannot but impinge on us all. It has proved difficult for many people to discover the art of remembering 'the People's Princess' who has been spoken about as much in her death as in her life. Not a day has passed without press attention focusing on her, her sons, her family and her friends. Disagreements over the forms of memorial, profiteering in tacky souvenirs, insensitive criticism and sincere devotion have all played a part in a country unwilling to let its most loved woman go. She radiated affection and compassion. The proper of way of remembering her is an art still to be found.

At the heart of both the Jewish religion and the Christian faith, the importance of remembering in an appropriate way is underlined. Because Jesus was a Jew, the essence of the former is carried over into the latter. It was at a Passover meal that Jesus instituted the great Christian act of remembrance, the Last Supper. The Jewish table-ceremony began with the blessing of the bread and ended with the common cup. To these elements of blessing and thanksgiving, taken into the Last Supper, Jesus added his instruction that the action would become a commemoration 'for as often as you eat this bread and drink this cup, you do show the Lord's death until he come'. Can we find, in this, the basic elements in the art of remembering?

There is first simplicity. Strip away all liturgical addi-

28. 1998

tions to Jesus's commemoration – whether it is described as Mass, Eucharist, Lord's Supper or Holy Communion – and the ritual is simple indeed. Take bread, take wine, give thanks and share. Remembering needs to be profound in its simplicity. Then there is sincerity, a factor emphasized by St. Paul in his instructions to the Corinthians about motivation, contained in his guidance on communion. Thirdly, grief must be personal. All will mourn, but each must do it in his or her own way. For some, a public demonstration of emotion will ease the strain. Others will cry their hearts out alone and in private. For some, ritual will be needed, but the temperaments of others may have no such need, for each one's grieving is unique in circumstance, tone and depth of feeling.

The anniversary of Diana's death, affecting each one of us in its own way, may bless us by helping us to find something of the art of remembering, and the invitation to commitment and compassion implicit in any true memorial.

Trivial Pursuits

'Live at the Church on Sunday' the poster proclaimed. Was this some important religious event – a choral concert? The presence of a great evangelist? A modern group presenting new forms of musical communication? An inter-faith dialogue? The full announcement in fact read: 'Live at the Church on Sunday – Arsenal v. Manchester United'.

The location, popularly known as 'the Church' was once a place of worship but is now a very large public house. A 'listed building', its exterior had to remain unaltered, but the sanctuary area was transformed into a very large modern pub. It was in that building that the live football match would be available on screen. A large congregation no doubt attended that act of worship, for 'act of worship' in some sense it was. Sport has become a popular religion. Its leading lights are worshipped (not only in words, but gestures) as god-like beings. Some well-known managers have been said (in an oblique reference to the one who came as Messiah) to 'walk on water'. And the liberality is huge. It has to be in order to pay wages, to its most outstanding participants, of sums in the region of £40,000 a week. That poster symbolized the superficiality of so much at the heart of contemporary society, the modern search for a substitute religion and the sheer triviality of so many contemporary pursuits.

It is frightening to realize that in the real world, the number of people who actually attended that match at the football ground is not dissimilar to the number who are believed to have died in the appalling earthquake in Turkey. When a geological fault and human failure combine to destroy the lives and livelihoods of thousands upon thousands of people, we are staring the realities of life in the face. It is here that the mystery of suffering tears at faith, delves deeply into doubt, and frames the questions that cannot be answered but seem to question the integrity of a God of love.

There is no good purpose served by the Church berating society for its trivial pursuits and tawdry ways. Far better that it should proclaim positively the truths it has received from the One who was listened to gladly in his time because he spoke with authority. The re-discovery of the authority of the Word, and the finding of ways to proclaim it 'with boldness' in today's world, remains a millennium priority.

There is no practical purpose served by the academic discussion of 'the problem of suffering'. Theological intricacies are of no immediate comfort to the distraught parent, the despairing partner or the crushed family. The need is for the compassion that reflects the loving heart of God.

The deep roots and firm foundations of faith lie in the experiences that teach and train the soul in faith and trust – the wonder of divine forgiveness and an unwavering conviction in the desire of God to bring wholeness and healing to the world.

Moral Progress?

Morality is prominent in public discussion as we approach the millennium. On the political agenda, it is also the focus of religious writing. Bishop Richard Holloway, in his most recent book, *Godless Morality* [29], making the case for 'a morality without God', describes his book as 'an attempt to offer a human-centred justification' for morality.

When the late Sir Malcolm Sargent was asked by a Nonconformist minister and author, Frank Jennings (popularly know as 'The Tramps' Parson'), 'In your opinion, is our nation progressing morally and spiritually?' he rather tartly replied that 'England today must surely be at its most immoral period in history'. That strong response was not reflected in the replies of other 'leading people'. Dame Sybil Thorndike wrote (all these quotations are from personal, but not private letters in front of me) an enthusiastic 'Yes! Yes! Yes!' and saw progress in the attitudes and activities of the younger generation. 'We are progressing', agreed Sir Richard Acland. 'The vast majority of English men and women have retained the moral and spiritual sense which has long been a national characteristic', wrote Christina Foyle. Others were less sure – Beverley Baxter was not confident: 'There has undoubtedly been a lowering of moral values since the end of the war . . . In political life, all the parties have concentrated almost solely on the material aspect of life and neglected the spiritual'. Vera Brittain wrote strongly: 'Morally and spiritually there has been a great deterioration in the higher places of our country. On the other hand there has been a great change for the better among ordinary people'. Lord Vansittart was definite: 'No, of course we are not progressing morally or spiritually. We are going backward – and how!'

29. *Godless Morality*, by Richard Holloway, Canongate Books, Edinburgh, 1999.

That was 1949. Fifty years further on, what would the responses to that same question be? Varied, no doubt, but many would probably feel that deterioration in both the moral and spiritual areas has increased. The two world wars and the ability of mankind to continue to inflict suffering through conflict, the love of power, the strength of selfishness and greed, the obsessive desire to acquire and possess, the abuse of the world's resources, the accumulation of the 'haves' and the poverty of the 'have-nots', have done much to erase beliefs in continuous progress, and re-emphasize the realities of the power of evil, latent and real, within humanity.

The coming of the millennium can serve a purpose if it compels us to have a personal spiritual stocktaking and a fresh look at the need for a true morality, godless or God-inspired. What we take into the new millennium are the traditions that are of lasting value plus an openness to new ideas in every part of life, not least theological and ecclesiastical, and a determination to forward the things that are good and lovely.

The new millennium points to new opportunities. Many will therefore say 'Let the renewing Spirit come!'

Wealth and Morality

Poverty is a gift and a grace, but only in one context, the self-chosen commitment of good people. Those who maintain vows of poverty deserve unstinted admiration. But poverty unsought, especially as in the horrendous examples of it certain parts of the world, is not only damaging to bodies. It also destroys minds and souls. It must therefore be as contrary to the will of God as anything can be. So also is the fear of poverty that stalks so many people today. The internationally agreed aim of reducing poverty by half by the year 2015 is, as Clare Short (the Secretary of State for International Development) says, 'a moral and environmental imperative'.

Wealth, too, can be threatening. The Psalmist puts it succinctly: 'Though your riches increase, set not your heart upon them' (Psalm 62:10). It is not money as such that is the root of evil. It is the love of money which is so subtly dangerous. Wealth can fundamentally change attitudes. Having much becomes wanting more. It is not surprising that Jesus said that it is not easy for a rich man to enter the kingdom of heaven.

The worrying connections between wealth and morality were also commented on in other ages. Seneca, the Roman writer, notes that 'money is the ruin of the true honour of things. We ask not what a thing truly is, but what it costs'. Juvenal, the satirical poet, describes money as 'the nurse of debauchery'. He goes on: 'No guilt or deed of lust is wanting since Roman poverty disappeared'. Paul wrote a withering criticism, in devastating detail, about that 'age of shame' in his letter to the Romans, calling it 'a situation of degeneracy of morals almost without parallel in human history' (William Barclay's translation). That this was not simply the view of a hysterical preacher is confirmed by his secular contemporaries.

There is much talk these days of the irrelevance of personal morality to political ability; of personal failure to political judgement. That question will continue to be debated. But the danger is that a belief is nourished that morality in public life does not matter at all. There follows the inevitable corollary that in an 'enlightened' world, spiritual attitudes are of no importance. If, however, both morality and spirituality are set aside, standards and values lose their traditional foundations. This results in a climate in which uncertainty and confusion grow. In some branches of the Church, indeed, anxiety and division are arising over particular pastoral problems in the field of sexuality. Many believe this to be the consequence of the erosion of biblical authority and traditional beliefs.

Degeneracy in Rome was countered by the proclamation of the gospel. The unique contribution of the Church is still its knowledge of the transforming power of God through grace. Its primary role today therefore remains the need to help the nation to flourish through the preaching of the Word. Changed people change situations. They did then. They can do today.

Time to Make Peace

'Some people think reconciliation is a soft option, that it means papering over the cracks. But the biblical meaning involves looking facts in the face. Reconciliation can be very costly.' The cost implicit in the ministry of reconciliation was certainly known to the author of these words, Desmond Tutu.

To be concerned with reconciliation is not one of the options religious people can select or reject. It is a commitment that is grounded in the very essence of the faith. In his second letter to the Corinthians, Paul spoke of the need to be 'Christ's ambassadors', carrying 'the message of reconciliation' as a prime responsibility because it flows from the very heart of the gospel. Because of our experience of God's reconciling love in Jesus, there is an obligation upon us to exercise a ministry of reconciliation to others. The ministry of reconciliation is rooted in the Incarnation. It is an obligation arising from the relationship restored by the saving acts of God.

Desmond Tutu's emphasis on the need to face the facts of any situation involving deep division must always be the first practical step in the ministry of reconciliation. The second must be the willingness of one party in the quarrel to take the first step in a reconciling endeavour. And moreover – and it is here that the element of cost is certainly present – to take that step while believing that the responsibility for that action should be on the other side.

A door with a hole cut out of it, on display in a church in Ireland, offers historic testimony to the potential fruitfulness of such an action. The hole was cut in the door by the head of one of two families locked in near-mortal combat, when the pursued leader found 'sanctuary' in the church. The pursuer cried to his enemy within the church to 'take his sword, cut a hole in the door and extend the hand of reconciliation'. But the pursued leader, questioning the integrity of the invitation, declined to take the suggested action. The pursuer then cried out that he himself would cut the hole in the door and extend his hand in reconciliation, to end the conflict. The hole in the door testifies to the action that was taken and the reconciliation that ensued, brought about by the pursuer (who was less obliged to do it) taking the first step.

There is no easy way to heal the hurt of family or domestic division; to bring healing to society; to lead the Church to a greater unity. Facile as it may seem to some, it needs to be remembered that Paul expounded his call to the ministry of reconciliation having just borne testimony to the fact that 'if anyone is in Christ, he/she is a new creation. The old has gone, the new has come'. Those who seek to reconcile the irreconcilable will always be believers in prayer and the transforming power of grace to bring new relationships into being.

IV. Healing Ministry

Unconditional Love

Evangelism and preaching should not concentrate on condemnation and judgement. The gospel in fact proclaims the unconditional love of God. At the heart of reality is the divine compassion expressed in a longing 'to seek and to save that which is lost'.

In Jesus's teaching method, the parable was used to indicate the attributes of God, to provide pictures illustrating the nature of the divine. The statement with which we began is founded not only on the specific Johannine words, making clear that God did not send his son into the world to condemn the world but to bring it salvation, but also on stories Jesus told about, for example, a lost sheep and a lost son. The first points to the divine initiative, the God who in compassion seeks the lost. The second demonstrates the welcome, love and grace that are expressed in unconditional joy over one who was lost and is found.

The prodigal son is a young man in the depths of misery. His money is spent. His dignity is destroyed. He longs, in his hunger, to share the pods put out for the pigs. Dispirited, devastated, desperate, he 'comes to himself' and sincerely and honestly prepares his confession. His sin is both against God and against his father. He no longer has the right to be considered a son. He must ask to be treated like one of the servants.

It is easy to picture the lost son rehearsing his speech on the journey back from the far country. He must take the initiative and pour out his confession. What happened was quite different! There was his father, already outside the house, waiting for him. And it was the latter who took the initiative, running to meet his son, throwing his arms around him in a warm embrace, kissing him rapturously. Did Jesus perhaps smile as he painted the picture of the lost son, trying to emerge from his father's embrace to pour out his planned words, almost to have them ignored? It is the father who takes the lead, sends for the best robe to put on his son, calls for sandals for his feet and a ring for his finger, and orders an immediate celebration. No doubt the confession, muffled by the embrace and drowned by the words of welcome, was heard, but far more important was the demonstration of unconditional welcome, unconditional grace and unconditional love offered by a father to his son. It is Jesus's picture of the love of God.

Repentance is a right, proper and necessary element in the restoring of the divine–human relationship, but the impact of the stories Jesus told lies in his demonstration of the divine initiative in reconciliation, and the yearning love of God for those who have chosen to go away. What a positive message lies at the centre of the gospel! What a marvellous insight is given into the nature of God!

Failure in Faith

He was a kindly man, a devoted pastor and a thoughtful preacher. A senior minister when I was just entering the ministry many years ago, I recall him still as a man of grace and goodness. In later years this minister had a life-threatening condition. In addition to orthodox medical help, he sought healing through the hands of the saintly author of *The Forgotten Talent*, Cameron Peddie, so great an influence in my own ministry. His condition, far from improving, deteriorated and, despite repeatedly praying for the miracle he believed would happen, he became increasingly ill. He died a bitter man. He had 'asked, believing' and had Jesus's assurance that 'he would receive'. He didn't and he was very angry about it.

There is a dilemma that those who take the healing ministry seriously feel very deeply. On one hand there is a lot about faith in the gospels, praise from Jesus for those who had faith, and rebuke for the disciples who failed to heal because of their 'unbelief', that is lack of faith. Jesus's message is clear: have faith, 'even as a grain of mustard seed'. To be 'of little faith' is to prevent a miracle. On the other hand, as has been demonstrated so often in public healing services or missions, the building up of huge expectations followed by failure to heal, results in real anguish. The resulting state may even be worse than the one that led to the search for a miracle.

The problem is not whether healing miracles occur or not. From my observation of others' experience, as from my own, they do. God is the God of surprises and 'wonderfull' things happen. Sometimes it will be through a combination of medical expertise and faith (for medicine is one of the gifts of creation for our healing); sometimes it will be more 'directly' in mysterious ways beyond our understanding. The problem comes when miracles prayerfully sought do not take place. The result can be devastation and bitterness.

There is a huge gap between what Jesus commands and what we achieve. Is it lack of faith? Or is it the low level of our spirituality? Jesus certainly seemed critical of his disciples' failure to learn from him. The miracle of the epileptic boy is placed by each gospel author immediately after the transfiguration and followed by Jesus's intimation of his coming death. But time is running out. ' How long shall I stay with you?' he asks, ' How long will I put up with you?' There is both disappointment and frustration because the disciples have so litttle faith. It only needs faith 'as a grain of mustard seed'. But there is a continuing gap.

The Church rightly involves itself with the problems of the world, be they political, economic or social. The primary task of the Church remains the obligation to deepen the spiritual power of people through bringing them into a closer relationship with Christ. It is through contact with him that spiritual power increases. The ability to reconcile, to change, to heal will only come through our 'closer walk with God'. Then, says Jesus, hard though it is to believe it, ' nothing will be impossible for you'.

The Healing Relationship

There is no doubt that in the past two weeks [30] the nation has undergone a profound spiritual experience, something no national mission could have achieved or evangelistic effort created. Hearts have been touched, minds have been changed, souls have been stirred, perhaps even restored by the contemplation, in one person, of the wonder of the healing relationship. For this is the essence of a ministry of compassion. Caring sensitivity and loving touch, offered to someone in need, brings profound healing.

This will be at the heart of the memories of Diana, Princess of Wales. And how gloriously that ministry of compassion was underlined in the coincidence of the death of Mother Teresa. That two people from such different backgrounds who knew, respected and loved each other, who were givers of life, should be united in death was surely a divine synchronicity of prophetic significance. It seemed to compel us all to be involved in the creation of a more compassionate society.

In the Bible, the classic presentation of the meaning of a healing relationship is the encounter of Jesus with the unpopular tax-gatherer Zacchaeus. In what becomes an acted-out parable, Jesus makes clear the key elements of the healing relationship, namely a 'moving towards', a 'being with' and the resultant 'going on'. The 'moving towards' comes from compassion. The 'being with' is expressed in sensitivity to need and empathy with suffering (outer or inner), the 'moving on' is the growth that comes from such a healing relationship. It is hard to think of two people who, in one brief week, so illuminated our understanding of a healing relationship.

30. Published just after the death of Diana, Princess of Wales, in August 1997.

But there is more to the spiritual experience that has touched virtually everyone. How many have said they would not have believed they could feel and act as they did? What they have seen and shared has created a self-awareness that has manifested itself in vibrant emotion, a readiness to cry, an enthusiasm to express feelings in flowers, written words, applause.

When Jesus met, talked to and befriended a Samaritan woman, the effect on her was dramatic. 'He told me all about myself', she said to her friends. A totally unplanned meeting, breaking religious protocol – for 'the Jews had no dealings with the Samaritans', the woman said – touched the depths of her being to the point of a conversion. So is it for us all. The experiences that transform us are so often seemingly accidental but with hindsight providential – an encounter with someone special, a combination of unusual circumstances, an involvement in tragedy. A dreadful happening two weeks ago has done something to a nation which means it will never be the same again.

Millions watched a service in a church. Thousands sang hymns and said prayers on city streets. Those who might well have denied they were in any way interested in the spiritual dimension were caught up in prayer, praise and dedication. And all because someone showed the meaning of the healing relationship. Within a dreadful tragedy there has been given a glorious gift for which we must all be grateful to God.

Sign of Health

Definitions of health have often been attempted, but seldom satisfactorily accomplished. For that very reason, it is helpful to turn to other concepts in order to try to illustrate what good health means. The word 'wholeness' is one popular synonym. It is a useful one, in that it sees health not simply as physical well-being but as health in every aspect of our being. Wholeness is the achievement of health not only in the body but also in the mind, the heart, the soul. In other words, to be healthy means demonstrating a wholeness that embraces the physical, mental, emotional and spiritual aspects of our being, and does so in their relationship with one another.

That concept, however, still needs other terms to convey its full impact and, in the quest for them, two words are particularly useful. One is harmony and the other is balance. If harmony means, as the dictionary defines it, 'the pleasing interaction or appropriate combination of the elements in a whole', a positive creative image is given for our understanding of wholeness. If balance is defined as 'a harmonious or satisfying arrangement of parts and elements', it too points to positive creative design or composition. The achievement of such harmony or balance will, or certainly should, be expressed in positive attitudes to the world around us and the people within it. A sign of health, in that total sense, is a commitment to 'love and serve the world'.

January, a traditional time for new beginnings, falls in the depths of winter, with its cold and dark days. It is a time when many feel depressed, and their depression may well be reflected in a jaundiced view of life and people. But a sense of reality about human nature should not lead to a negative view of life and people. There is so much that is positive and creative in the world.

The spiritual writer Thomas Merton seems, in his autobiography *The Seven Storey Mountain*, to reflect a very negative attitude to the world, revealing a manifest distaste for its ways before he went into the monastery at Gethsemane in 1941. Having left the monastery in 1948, his attitude has become much more positive. 'I met the world and found it no longer wicked after all', he writes. 'Perhaps the things I resented about the world when I left it were defects of my own that I projected upon it . . . I went through the city, realizing for the first time in my life how good are all the people in the world and how much value they have in the sight of God.'

'God sent not his son into the world to condemn the world, but that the world through him might be saved.' There is no statement more positive and creative than that. It may well be a sign of improving health when we find we are more ready to 'love and serve the world' with all our being.

Healing Power

One of the most exciting developments in the life of the Church over the last two decades is the recovery of the healing ministry as a fundamental part of the presentation of the gospel. In so many churches across the denominations, services offering blessing by the laying on of hands are a normal part of the church's worship programme. Many would see this development as a work of the Holy Spirit.

Most such services are liturgical in their emphasis, and rightly so. All services should of course be healing, but to have a particular context in which the ministry to wholeness is visibly expressed in symbolic action is certainly another means of grace. Laying on of hands, a prominent biblical practice associated with the giving of power in both the Old and New Testaments, can be an energizing sign and seal of the promise of God to seek wholeness in body, soul, mind and spirit for all people.

In some churches, a counselling component is introduced into healing ministry services, but not happily. To have spiritual counselling available after the service itself (in an appropriate place) is proper but, for both personal and practical reasons, it is not helpful in a public situation. Confining the action to a purely liturgical one is more appropriate. It is a proclamation to all, recipients and congregation, of the healing power of Jesus. The word 'power' is important. It was this healing power that Jesus used in whatever method he applied to individual needs. As the doctor–evangelist Luke noted: 'The power of the Lord was present to heal'. The question then arises as to whether healing power is actually transmitted in the act of laying on of hands? In Jesus's time it was. That it still is, where people minister in his name, is the conviction of many.

There are those who think that being able to touch holy things, such as a relic, an icon or other religious symbol, can

127

bring about a healing miracle. There was certainly a belief that being able to touch Jesus could have such an effect. Is this belief or superstition? The authoritative answer is given by Jesus himself in the incident where a woman with a long-standing uterine haemorrhage ('an issue of blood for twelve years') succeeded in touching one of the tassels of his cloak. It was for her not superstition but an act of faith (as Jesus recognized when saying 'Your faith has made you whole'). Still more important is the fact that Jesus confirms that power (*dunamis*) has gone out of him. 'The woman was healed by the power of God which was available in Jesus', writes John Wilkinson, a medical doctor. He continues: 'This was the power which Jesus used in every method he used for healing'. [31]

Medicine and healing ministry are both God-given and complementary to each other. I suspect that many a doctor or surgeon would testify that where healing power unites with medical or surgical skill, the possibilities of a miracle are immense. There are certainly those who have so benefited who would testify to the wonder of such co-operation.

31. *Health and Healing, Studies in New Testament Principles and Practice,* by John Wilkinson, Handsel Press, 1980.

From Death to Life

For weeks the patient lay in the intensive care ward, holding on to life by a thread – or rather the wires that led to the support machines around his bed. Under heavy sedation for further weeks, he remained to all intents unconscious. I was there when the consultant said the position was 'desperate'. It was underlined by the expressed need to move towards a decision to withdraw such life support.

It is always dangerous to discuss a patient's problems round the bed in such circumstances. The hearing faculty, it has been suggested, is the last one to go. Patients, though deeply unconscious, may hear what is being said about them – as happened in this case. As my friend told me, after his astonishing return from death to life – a product of superb medical care and, perhaps, the bedside service that had been suggested to his wife by one of the nurses – of his hearing a member of the medical team say to colleagues as they studied his 'desperate' situation: 'If I were him, I would just let go.' His inner response was immediate and clear as he heard himself saying: 'No, I am going to live.'

There are miraculous recoveries from near-death to new life and this is one of them. Three factors seemed to be involved in the miracle. First there was the extraordinary level of medical expertise and technology. That is in itself part of the miracle of modern medicine. The second was the presence of the faith and prayers of believing family and friends. The third was the patient's will to win. The miracle lies, surely, in a combination of all three. The spontaneous joy and admiration of the medical staff seemed to testify to the miracle too.

It is unwise to be oversimplistic in talking about healing miracles, but in this still-evolving story there lies encouragement to those who wrestle with illness and feel fatalistic forces at work. Medicine, faith and will make a potent treatment.

From the miracles Jesus worked on the man 'sick of the palsy' who was let down through the roof and the 'impotent' man who had waited a long time to get into the pool by the temple, it seems clear that he recognized that the causes of illness included emotional or spiritual factors. In both cases Jesus effected the physical cure, but he also stressed the need for something in addition to physical healing. In the case of the palsied young man, he not only cured his condition but emphasized his need for forgiveness. To the impotent man he issued a stern warning: 'If you don't change your lifestyle,' he said in effect, 'your illness will return and next time it will be worse.'

It is not only disease of the body that needs treatment. It is the dis-ease that affects mind, heart and spirit that also needs the healing touch.

Creative Compassion

I cannot walk along Edinburgh's Princes Street, past the tall monument to Sir Walter Scott without remembering – and yet it is so very long ago – a good man, a devoted pastor of many years in a parish just outside the city, who threw himself to his death from the top of that monument. Ruddy and cheerful of countenance, gracious in manners, gifted in the pulpit – and yet for some reason it happened. The anguish behind that decision is painful to imagine.

I passed that monument only a few days ago. The sight of it, with its memories, took me back to a sermon preached in St. Paul's Cathedral some time ago. The occasion was the Festival of the Sons of the Clergy, a situation that moved the preacher, the Very Revd Michael Mayne, to tell of his own father's death. 'On a Saturday afternoon in May, my father wrote a note to my mother who was out, climbed the tower of the church beside the rectory, removed the boarding from the belfry and threw himself down. He died almost immediately.'

It is never right, as I have said before, to say to anyone who has gone through torment or suffered tragedy 'I know how you feel.'* All experience is unique. If you have never lost a child, it is impossible to know what such an experience is truly like. For the same reason, only those who have taken their own lives can know the anguish that leads to such a drastic decision. It is a time when nothing you have ever believed in seems to have any relevance to you and the situation in which you find yourself.

At the time when Michael Mayne's father's died – some 60 years ago – he tells us that a suicide was not allowed a proper burial, marked grave or memorial. The coroner at the inquest commented: 'I cannot conceive of a clergyman

* see Meditation number 48

desecrating holy ground, as Mr Mayne has done'. And, adds Michael Mayne, 'no one ever spoke of my father again'.

From the parish in which Mr Mayne senior had served, almost a lifetime later, has come a statement by the rector that 'we would like to see a simple memorial to him erected'. This has duly taken place. It is a kind of healing of which Michael Mayne said in his sermon: 'We and the local body of Christ, which are my father's parish, are saying to him: "We shall never know why you did what you did, for that is known only to you and to God; but your desperate cry for help came out of so much anguish of spirit that it demands not our judgement but our compassion".'

It is in line with the spirit of the Master that his followers, when faced by events they cannot accept or understand, should choose not the rigours of judgement, but the creative power of compassion. If such an attitude is considered a risk to standards and values, it is nevertheless the risk we need to take.

V. Times and Seasons

A Meditation for Lent: 'Deare Lent'

'Welcome, deare Feast of Lent!' wrote George Herbert. It is a cry so vigorous and enthusiastic that it compels reflection on the meaning of the Lenten season. There are those who associate Lent with doom and gloom, denial and self-negation, unwelcome and restrictive discipline, yet for others, like that poet priest in the seventeenth century, Lent is a celebration. Perhaps no season in the Christian year so attracts both negative attention and positive proclamation. Lent is fasting and feasting, discipline and delight, pancakes and pilgrimage, burden and blessing. Lent is, like love, a many-splendoured thing. It is rightly welcome.

Associated with the Lenten season are many facets of the faith and the spiritual life. Its primary link is with spring, so it points positively to new beginnings. In the early Church, Lent was linked with training for discipleship. It was associated with forgiveness and reconciliation, consciously expressed in the receiving back into communion of true penitents. The journey from Ash Wednesday to Easter is a pilgrimage profoundly touched by the sufferings of the Lord. It is the search for 'whole-souled loveliness' (as a Celtic blessing describes it) in journeying with Jesus through the pain of Calvary, the gross darkness of the descent into hell and the glory of the Garden of the Resurrection. 'Deare Lent' is then welcome not as a time of giving something up (though that is a useful discipline) but of grasping something new and life-giving. Its prime purpose is the pursuit of holiness. 'There is nothing negative or killjoy about holiness', the late David Watson assures us. Mother Teresa puts it in a marvellously positive and exciting way: 'Holiness consists in doing the will of God . . . with a smile'.

But there are times when it is hard to smile, including now. Horrific pictures of human tragedy in Mozambique push our ability to watch and absorb it to the limit, as the sight of suffering surely as awful as any of us have ever seen is brought into our safe and comfortable homes. It is suffering on a scale so vast and unbelievable – as was the Holocaust sixty years ago. We cannot travel the Lenten way without facing, yet again, the sheer mystery of suffering. Yet at the same time we are in the company of him who turned death into life, defeat into victory, hopelessness into hope. Welcome, deare Lent, for your coming takes us to the deep places where the worst has to be encountered while we are assured that the best is yet to be.

'Practical holiness and entire self-consecration to God are not sufficiently attended to by modern Christians in this country.' That was said even before the twentieth century began, by the famous Anglican, Bishop Ryle. If it is equally true today, then let the world – but not least the Church – welcome deare Lent and its invitation to travel on the Lenten road to holiness. And to do it, if it is possible, with a smile.

A Meditation for Lent:
Towards Maturity

On Jesus's journey towards Jerusalem, and during the events that happened there, characters of whom little is known played minor but positive parts on his behalf. There was, for example, Simon of Cyrene.

Cyrene, in Libya, was the home of numerous Jews. They shared with others a synagogue in Jerusalem (the Book of Acts tells us) so Simon, not unnaturally, was there to celebrate the Passover. All we know about him, however, is in the one verse which each of the Synoptic Gospels allocates to him. Mark, whose gospel was based on memories of the dictated words of Peter, does mention that Simon had two sons, Alexander and Rufus, giving the impression he was known to the disciples. But that is about all. Each simply records that Simon of Cyrene was enlisted by the Roman soldiers (as they had the 'legal right' to do) to carry Jesus's cross when he stumbled, exhausted, under its weight.

Interesting too is the otherwise unmentioned wife of Pilate who, with a woman's intuition and following unpleasant daydreams, 'begged' her husband to 'have nothing to do with that just man'. History has recorded her personal plea on Jesus's behalf when all around seemed hell-bent on destroying him.

This is the sinister element in the journey towards Calvary and one which no individual intervention could contain. Corporate pressure and institutional prejudice on the part of the authorities (and not least the religious authorities) had taken over. The strength of the forces of hostility is expressed in the pathetic ritual of Pilate washing his hands of responsibility. There was by now a tidal wave of uninformed, uncritical, unjust corporate antipathy, determined to bring about the destruction of Jesus. This is indeed a frightening example of the corporate 'shadow', that interplay of irrational negative feelings which no rational argument can contain. It leads towards the public choosing the release of the murderer Barabbas, rather than that of the innocent Christ. What greater sin could there be than this!

Corporate hostility, in the form of institutional prejudice, still afflicts society. We would all, if asked, make clear our dislike of racism and violence; however deep, hidden, unrecognized (unconscious) feelings can, under pressure of circumstances, be ignited by believed threats to territory and possessions.

Lent is a time for confession, repentance, reconciliation and spiritual regeneration, the acknowledgement of our need to face the negative forces that spoil our lives and, too often, the lives of others. Lent is the 'inner springtime', the time for re-creation.

Lin Berwick (in a quite different context, but not irrelevantly to our theme) has said in writing of her severe disabilities (cerebral palsy, blindness and wheelchair user): 'I have tried to take the negative of disability, stand it on its head and make it positive and beautiful for God'.* The Lenten 'spring-clean' – in which all that is negative is thus changed into that which is positive and beautiful for God – will advance our spiritual maturity, deepen our faith and make us more of a blessing to others.

* In a Lin Berwick Trust Newsletter (TLBT, 4 Chaucer Road, Sudbury, Suffolk CO10 1LN).

A Meditation for Lent:

Inner Springtime

'It is not only the will to win that is necessary,' said the athlete, who had just broken a long-distance world record, 'it is the will to prepare.' It is a thought relevant to the season of Lent. The spiritual journey involves the discipline of preparation.

Lent, in the early Church, had strong connections with preparation. It was the time set aside for the teaching and training of baptismal candidates. But the Lenten discipline was not confined to them. Church members, too, were exhorted to engage in spiritual practices, especially praying, fasting and studying, and to do so with humility. A sense of the importance of a period of focused spiritual discipline, as a preparation for the remembrance of the sufferings of Jesus and the wonders of the resurrection, rightly continues today. Journeying with Jesus through his wilderness and along the Lenten way, in sincerity and with humility, is found by most pilgrims to enrich the spiritual life. 'Travelling together' (the theme of one Lenten address in the current [32] series in York Minster, led by Sisters of the Holy Paraclete) aptly describes the significance of the Lenten journey.

Lent is a time of positive spiritual endeavour involving the discipline of preparation and leading to the discovery of new life. It is here that its association with spring becomes excitingly relevant. Even now, as that season approaches, shoots and buds proclaim new life, renewal, creation and re-creation. Lent is our inner springtime. It is not a time to dwell gloomily on our failures, our darkness, our spiritual inadequacy (though a healthy recognition of our weakness is appropriate). It is a time to point to the potential for our growth towards

32. 1999.

spiritual maturity, if we travel with the Lord on his journey towards Jerusalem and all that lay at the end of it.

'This day may I reconnect with the springtime within me', prays the author of the section 'Inner Springtime' in *Catching the Dream*. [33] The writer goes on: 'In our inner preparation for the great festival of Easter, we need to balance the focus in our shortcomings with a focus on the springtime within us. Whatever our chronological age, we each have an inner child within that longs to be invited out to play, to skip like the lambs, to express the creativity that the child finds so natural and the adult so often finds blocked by inhibitions'. So the true Lent speaks of hope, of spiritual progress, of the new creation for ever possible through grace.

'For heaven's sake – keep on' is the final title in the York series referred to above. Lent involves the discipline of preparation and the determination to keep going, to 'run the race that is before us . . . looking unto Jesus' for he is our inspiration on the Lenten journey and our companion on a pilgrimage through suffering to victory.

33. *Catching the Dream, New Start for the Millennium*, a Lenten study published by ACTS, Scottish Churches House, Dunblane, Scotland FK15 OAJ, 1999.

A Meditation for Lent: Jesus Wept

In the gospels, it is not recorded that Jesus laughed, only that he wept. When he learned of the death of his friend, Lazarus, and felt deeply the sorrow of Lazarus's sisters, Martha and Mary, the tears flowed. That emotional reaction to his bereavement proclaimed his true humanity. Described variously as 'God incarnate', 'the Word made flesh' even 'God with us', here was a true human being who knew the meaning of grief, could feel others' pain and was able to weep over his and their loss. What a momentous declaration of the divine empathy with every distraught soul!

St. John, at the end of his gospel, underlines how little we know of what Jesus said and did. 'Jesus did many other things as well', he writes, adding enthusiastically: 'If every one of them were written down, I suppose that even the whole world would not have room for the books that would be written'. Perhaps amusing events are among those that went unrecorded.

The Lenten journey is not primarily a time for laughter. It is a time of pain. The road towards Jerusalem will end with the agony of crucifixion. It will become the way of suffering to which Jesus always knew his obedience would lead. Even as a twelve-year-old boy he had bemused his parents by declaring, in seeming rebuke, that he 'must be about his father's business'. Following Peter's confession: 'You are the Christ, the Son of the living God', he deliberately began to explain to his disciples 'that he must go to Jerusalem – and be killed'. Moved by the picture of the suffering servant so dramatically portrayed by the prophet Isaiah, he recognized that he would be despised and rejected, a man of sorrows acquainted with grief. But it was not only physical suffering he anticipated. He would become too the victim of institutional prejudice on the part of 'elders, priests and teachers of the law'. He would face the conflict between self-interesst and obedience in the Garden of Gethsemane. He would even cry from the cross in utter dereliction: 'My God, my God, why have you forsaken me?'

It is precisely Jesus's experience of suffering that is his greatest gift to troubled people. His tears for Lazarus speak with love to the bereaved partner or parent. His agony as he faced the conflict between a longing for life and the need to give it up will touch the heart of those who want to live but contemplate their self-destruction. His own distress over the seeming absence of God, in his darkest hour, will strike a chord with those who, at their wits' end, cannot feel the divine presence at all.

Jesus wept. Those who travel the Lenten way in his company can only be grateful that, sharing human pain, he suffered as he did. To all who weep, agonize and mourn, the tears of Jesus make real the sympathy of God.

A Meditation for Lent: For Everyman

'Lord, is it I?' What drama is encapsulated in that cry uttered, virtually in unison, by the disciples! It happened at the Passover meal, the meal that was to become the Last Supper. There he made the statement that bewildered and saddened the disciples: 'One of you shall betray me'. It was then that 'every one of them' asked that uncomfortable question, anxiously questioning their behaviour and attitudes without understanding why they felt guilty. Each in his heart wondered if he had failed in his discipleship.

The journey of Jesus towards Jerusalem, Calvary and the Garden of the Resurrection has always aroused emotion and passion, and has led to so much great music which, this and every Easter, will draw crowds not only to cathedrals and churches, but to concert halls of many kinds. The events of Holy Week touch the minds, hearts and souls of millions. The sheer greatness of a good man (whether or not he can be called Saviour and Lord), the unfairness and injustice of his appalling suffering, the sense of his involvement with people in their pain (because he understood it through sharing it), touch a human nerve and create a spontaneous response. There is a sense in which Jesus belongs to the whole world and deep down the world acknowledges it. If it cannot bring itself to say 'my Lord and my God' as Thomas did, it may well say '*Ecce homo*', 'Behold the man'.

There is an irony in the nature of the responses to Jesus's suffering. Often his followers failed him. Yet strangers supported him. Judas's betrayal, foreseen and prophesied by Jesus, led to his self-inflicted death, an act of remorse and profound guilt. Peter's denial was also foretold by Jesus. The tears Peter shed reflected his sense of failure. There was corporate failure, too, at the time of Jesus's arrest: 'All the disciples forsook him and fled.'

But there were positive responses to Jesus from people outside the category of formal discipleship. There was Joseph of Arimathea, a secret disciple, and a member of the Sanhedrin, the court of justice that tried Jesus. Did Joseph protest? Was he present when Jesus was condemned? Was he another failure? But he did redeem himself and pay his own tribute by receiving Jesus's body from Pilate and giving it a seemly burial. There was the centurion on guard by the cross who felt moved to cry in tribute: 'Surely this man was a son of God'. There was the penitent thief, ready to acknowledge the innocence of Jesus and seek his blessing. There was Pilate's wife, imploring her husband not to be involved in the death of 'that innocent man'. All came, in some way, from the world outside his circle, to acknowledge and honour a good man.

And so the man from Nazareth belongs both to the Church and to the world. If not everyone feels able to 'crown him Lord of all', each can offer thanks, praise and admiration in his or her own way for the man.

A Meditation for Lent: Road to Holiness

Lent is not a time for dreariness. It is a time for the development of the spiritual life; a time for journeying with Jesus and therefore making proper preparation for Easter; a time for reflection on what it means to be in, but not of, the world; a time for meditating on the need, paradoxical though it sounds, both to separate (for separateness is an essential element in holiness) and to be involved (which the doctrine of the Incarnation demands); a time for sharing in Jesus's suffering and preparing to rejoice in his resurrection. Lent is a time when the hope of an enhanced spirituality is high. This makes it an opportunity.

High hopes and hard spiritual realities come into conflict when we try to be in, but not of, the world. Spirituality must always be earthed in reality lest it becomes false piety or sheer escapism. There is a connection between faith and actions, for feelings of faith must be expressed in acts of love. Those spiritual eyes that 'gaze up into heaven' can be allowed only to those whose feet are firmly on the ground. The necessity of a lively spiritual life is stressed by Michael Ramsey when he comments: 'A church which starves itself and its members in the contemplative life deserves whatever spiritual leanness it experiences'. The 'longest journey in the world,' writes Dag Hammarskjold, 'is the journey inwards'. But he goes on: 'The road to holiness inevitably goes through the world of action'. It is imperative that we touch and handle things unseen. It is equally imperative that we serve the widow and the orphan in their affliction. That, says James, in his New Testament letter, is genuine religion.

There is, as Ezra Pound said of his times, a 'tawdry cheapness' about the world today. Opportunism, not opportunity, characterizes its life. The world of publishing has been shown to be like so much else, driven by the money market. So increasingly is the world of sport. Mega-mergers dominate the financial news, as ever bigger units are deemed to be essential to economic survival. The lottery brings hope to the people – or, more likely for most, despair. How hard it is to attend to the spiritual life when we are so focused on Mammon. It may be part of the responsibility of our personal and corporate Lenten reflection to take notice of the reminder from Jesus at the time of his temptation: 'Man does not live by bread alone'. Life must be built on the solid rock of a living faith, not the shifting sands of shares and dividends.

'Wherein lies happiness?' asks John Keats in 'Endymion'. His answer? 'In that which becks our ready minds to fellowship divine'. 'Happiness,' said the blind and deaf Helen Keller 'is not obtained through self-gratification but through fidelity to a worthy purpose'. If Lent can bring us benefit, it may well be through the grasping of the opportunity to realize anew the validity of the claim of virtually every faith that it is the things which are not seen that are lasting, yet ultimately immensely practical.

A Meditation for Mothering Sunday:
A Mother's Heart

My mother went to school with D. H. Lawrence. She said later: 'He was a very strange young man'. She was a disciplined Victorian lady, so her reaction to him was not really surprising. She was trained by a strict father, whose stern personality was evidenced by the way he treated his only son. For some misdemeanour, he was expelled from the family home for ever. He went abroad and was never seen again (though my mother did maintain a correspondence with him). My mother, an artist and a musician, accepted the discipline in which she had been schooled. Lawrence, keen to extend the boundaries of current thought and behaviour, was not a natural soulmate for her.

Mothering Sunday has stimulated these reflections on the questions that my mother's passing reference to Lawrence raised. They focus on the concepts of discipline and freedom. Not mutually hostile, they can be so when each is taken to an extreme. Discipline (not in my mother's case, but possibly in her father's) can descend into judgementalism and dogmatism. Freedom, if it is abused, becomes not liberty but licence. Because we live in the 'anything goes' society, entertainment constantly reflects the desire to push the boundaries of acceptance further and further. At the beginning of the twenty-first century, isn't there a greater need for personal and public self-discipline, less irresponsibility and more responsibility, less violence, cruelty and brutality?

Jesus's mother, Mary, was human. When Jesus went missing in the temple in Jerusalem, her annoyance with him for giving his parents anxiety was clear. She was distressed but dignified as her son was crucified, and she was loyal to his cause by being involved in the disciples' post-Ascension meetings. But there was in her too a profound humility and spiritual sensitivity. What she said, on realizing her calling as the mother of one who would 'redeem Israel', cannot help but move: 'I am the Lord's servant. Be it unto me according to your will.'

Mary journeyed with Jesus through tragedy to triumph. The former was not unexpected, for had not Simeon told her, when he gave thanks for Jesus, that 'a sword would pierce through her own heart too'? From then on she was involved in events she could not understand. What she had was the capacity to 'keep all these things' – the puzzling words, the surprising actions (as at the marriage in Cana) – and 'ponder them in her heart'. It was an act of faith and of commitment beyond the bounds of maternal responsibility.

'The loveliest masterpiece in the heart of God,' said the nineteenth-century Carmelite nun, Thérèse of Lisieux, 'is the heart of a mother'. Mary is surely the incarnation of that truth. In an all too heartless and cruel world, let us give thanks for the dignity, self-discipline and sensitivity of Mary, and for the gentle graces of women. The world greatly needs them.

A Meditation for Passion Sunday:
Holy Passion

After Jesus's triumphal entry into Jerusalem, some Greeks went to the disciple Philip with the plea: 'Sir, we would like to see Jesus'. The action somehow expresses the need for some kind of a saviour. So often people sought out Jesus; Nicodemus, the Pharisee, by night, secretly; Zacchaeus, the despised tax-gatherer, up a tree, openly; the crowds, pursuing him when he needed a quiet place with his disciples. And so it has been down the ages. Those who 'hunger and thirst after righteousness' have sought him out to learn from him as a teacher, to be made whole by him as a healer, to be inspired by him as a preacher, to be drawn to him as the supreme example for living.

'He came unto his and his own received him not' yet, nearly two millennia later, his name is universally spoken, his words revered and his teaching treasured by millions. He was 'despised and rejected', and yet his name is honoured not only within the religion he founded, but in others as well. For some he will simply be the carpenter of Nazareth, to be honoured as a human being unique in goodness, proclaiming a profound but simple message about a way of life. To others he will be God incarnate in human life, who 'by his holy passion and his endless love' offers the salvation so needed by a corrupt world. Some will see him as the cosmic Christ who 'in the beginning was the Word and the Word was with God and the Word was God'. Here surely is the magnetism that draws seekers, searchers and sinners to him. In whatever way, at whatever level, he 'being lifted up' draws people to him. In whatever language each finds it appropriate, relevant, traditional, contemporary, academic, simple, every one can say 'May Jesus Christ be praised!' The Church may be deemed irrelevant by those outside it and many within it, but the 'king and head of the Church' never will be. In every time and every age there are those who will say with longing, hope and expectation 'We would like to see Jesus'.

When Mary Magdalene went to the Garden of the Resurrection, she cried broken-heartedly: 'They have taken away my Lord and I don't know where they have laid him'. Is this, metaphorically, the theme at the heart of recent accusations (made from within the Church about the irrelevance of the Church) that the essential Jesus, to whom so many have been, are and will be drawn, has been taken and hidden in unnecessary ritual, theological confusion, ecclesiastical minutiae, tedious assemblies, synods and conferences, the pursuit of personal power, the trivia of personal failings, and disunity round altar and table?

We are not told if the Greeks did meet Jesus, but his answer to the disciples through whom the request was conveyed was to say that his hour had come, and to point to his passion, for him the core of his mission. As Passion Sunday comes round again, it is for us all to keep 'looking unto Jesus', his holy passion and his endless love.

A Meditation for Passion Sunday:
Dignity in Suffering

'Mary, you are specially dear to God!' So William Barclay translates the salutation of the angel who came to announce to the mother of our Lord that she would bear the child Jesus. Her cousin, Elizabeth, was the first to underline how special Mary was, and down the ages that sense of respect for Mary has continued. Ecclesiastical traditions may vary in the nature of the place given to Mary, but what all can share is admiration for the quality of her womanhood and motherhood. 'I am the Lord's servant. Whatever you say, I accept', said Mary to the angel. It is her profound humility and vibrant obedience that makes her special.

On Passion Sunday, we reach the point in Lent when the suffering that Jesus had to face begins to impinge heavily on us. But it is Mary's torment too. Her dignity, in facing the suffering of her son and the pain it brought to her own heart, is moving beyond belief. Could there be anything more awful for a mother than having to watch her son being nailed to a cross, totally innocent of any crime, yet crucified with criminals? How could any woman bear such acquaintance with grief? Yet the record, if brief, is touching indeed. 'Jesus's mother . . . standing beside the cross.' In the hour of his extremity, she was there.

The Norwegian sculptor, Gustav Vigeland, has among his hundreds of sculptures a remarkable commentary on responses to suffering. The snow was deep in Oslo as Jillian and I stood in Vigeland's Sculpture Park, the very bleakness of winter seeming to underline the burden of life depicted in his sculpture of six life-size male figures, supporting a large saucer-shaped basin, which holds 'the water of life'. The figures express, by their attitudes and postures, the sheer effort involved in bearing life's suffering. Some seem to be near to coping. Others, weighed down and crushed, are finding life and its pain a burden 'grievous and heavy to be borne'. It is life as we all know it. Some cope better than others. Some struggle not to go under. Some cannot manage at all. There are those who are ground down by the mystery of suffering, puzzled over 'the bad things that happen to good people'. There are those who are the victims of the seemingly irrational and unfair distribution of suffering, and feel resentment and bitterness at the endlessness of their pain. But there are those too who are able to sense the creative possibilities of their suffering, and are able to grow in grace and maturity through their experience of life. How blessed they are!

Mary, with the dignity of her suffering, is an inspiration to us all as we struggle to cope with life. Mary, with her gentle graces, is remembered on Mothering Sunday, and it is worth recalling that that particular Sunday is also known as Refreshment Sunday. It is refreshment indeed to be encouraged by one who, dignified in suffering, was 'specially dear to God'.

A Meditation for Holy Week:
Good Centurions

How fascinating it is to realize that so many of the Roman centurions mentioned in the New Testament are presented in such a favourable light! Although they were soldiers in the army of an occupying foreign power, they are referred to with respect; each one shows an unexpected measure of sympathy with Jesus, or with his servant, Paul. There was the centurion Cornelius, who was used to help Peter to understand the inclusiveness of the gospel. There was the centurion who prevented soldiers taking Paul's life when he was shipwrecked on Malta. Another centurion cared for Paul when he was on trial before the governor, Felix. Yet another, having learned of a Jewish plot to murder Paul, did what he could to foil the attempt. And there was the centurion who, on suddenly discovering that Paul was a Roman citizen, saved him from the mob. Good centurions indeed!

At the time of Jesus's crucifixion, a particular reference demonstrates a sympathy and sensitivity so lacking in those responsible for his death. 'Surely,' cried the centurion on guard-duty near the cross, 'this was a righteous man'. It was a tribute, not from the religious community, but from the world outside it.

That pattern was much repeated in the life of Jesus. The penitent thief sensed the innocence and goodness of his companion on Calvary. 'This man has done nothing wrong', he declared boldly. It was a tribute the ecclesiastical establishment had refused to make. 'Do not have any thing to do with this innocent man', pleaded Pontius Pilate's wife as her husband sought to wash his hands of Christ. It was a warning from the secular world to which the religious community was blind. Jesus was a good man, constantly harassed, consistently accused, and finally condemned to death by orthodox religion, yet seen as a friend by 'publicans and sinners', as a prophet by a woman from Samaria, as a healer by a woman from Syrian Phoenicia. Those without formal training in spiritual disciplines somehow sensed the wonder of Jesus. Pharisees could descend as far as to accuse him of working miracles through the power of Beelzebub. What perversity is this! This is, for all involved in formal religion, a cautionary tale. His rejection should not have happened then, but it did. It ought not to happen now, but it could. If Christ is to be proclaimed to the world, the body created to do that must engage, not least in Lent, in a searching examination of its own faith, priorities and purpose. Those concerned formally or professionally with religion can be diverted from the heart of the faith by obsession with theological niceties, liturgical details, over-concern with organization and structure, maintenance rather than ministry, and in so doing hurt the world by taking away the Lord and forgetting where they have laid him. 'If the light that is in you is darkness,' Jesus said ominously, 'how great is that darkness'. It could after all 'crucify the Son of God afresh and put him to public shame'.

A Meditation for Holy Week:

Passion's Priorities

The word 'passion' has several meanings. One of them relates to Jesus's suffering. As Holy Week approaches, his Passion is, properly, a focus for reflection. But passion also means 'an abandoned display of emotion, especially of anger', while a third meaning is 'strong sexual desire'.

Was Jesus a passionate man? So far as the last dictionary definition is concerned, Jesus does not seem to have been passionate, certainly from the records that we have. This does not mean that the affection he felt for close friends – Lazarus, Mary of Bethany, Mary Magdalene – was not profound. It is simply noting that passion, in the sexual sense of the word, was not a demonstrated part of his life. Taking the word 'passionate' in the sense of 'emotional reaction', however, the story is quite different. Told of the death of Lazarus, and the sorrow of his friend's sisters, Mary and Martha, the tears flowed and Jesus wept. Other events made Jesus very angry and led him to act with passion –these involved insincere religion and disrespect for God.

The disciples, like the experts in the Law and some Pharisees mentioned in the story of 'the woman taken in adultery', had difficulty in knowing how Jesus would respond to situations. The latter group of people demonstrated that uncertainty in seeking his reaction to adultery. Producing the woman 'caught in the very act', they expected a passionate defence of the law of Moses on a matter which demanded stoning as the appropriate punishment. No such display came, and the silently retreating line of accusers, led by the eldest, indicated their failed expectations.

A similarly strong response seemed to be expected from Jesus over another 'woman that was a sinner'. As she washed Jesus's feet with her tears and dried them with her hair in a genuine act of love, the host, Simon the Pharisee, railed at the one who claimed to be a prophet but apparently did not know the woman's unacceptable background. The disciples too grumbled 'with indignation' at the waste of expensive ointment. Would Jesus share in such criticisms of either the woman or the waste? Certainly not. Simon was rebuked, and the woman commended.

It is clear then that it was not the personal peccadilloes, the 'sins of the flesh' that aroused Jesus's passion. But there is no doubt what did – the sins of spiritual arrogance, of self-righteousness and of hypocrisy, especially when shown by the official representatives of religion. The disrespect shown to God by temple consumerism and individual greed also moved him to passion. Money-changers and traders were driven out of the temple, their tables overturned. He used strong language too to condemn the 'play-actors' on the religious stage. 'Woe to you hypocrites', he said. It was this kind of sin that aroused Jesus's passion.

'Passion, I see, is catching', says Mark Antony in Shakespeare's *Julius Caesar*. The response to Jesus's Passion can only be the passionate pursuit of the things that were important to him. These surely include human rights for all, the expression of the value of every soul in having the right to fulfil its potential, and the effort to replace corporate and financial greed with the simpler values of the One who had no place to lay his head.

A Meditation for Easter:
Ascent from Hell

'I now know what hell is like', said a Serbian mother speaking after a night of bombing in Belgrade. The same cry of despair could equally come from the innocents who suffer in the killings of Kosovo, where civilians have been used as human shields in front of Serbian tanks, and in Albania, where 'killing is a stark reality'. The language of the conflict in the Balkans seems to reflect a descent into hell – 'unstoppable killings', 'reported executions', 'refugees in their thousands', 'the biggest human disaster in Europe since World War II'. It is the burden of human suffering that brings the stark realities of war and of the cross together. The suffering servant was a man of sorrows, acquainted with grief. In being 'God with us' he will surely weep over the pain of the world until the ascent from hell can come.

The descent into hell, remembered between Good Friday and Easter Day, is very important. The two specific references to it in the New Testament give no clear guidance to its meaning, but spiritual sensitivity recognizes its glorious significance. It points to the completeness of Christ's saving act. There is no depth beyond the reach of the divine love. No one can, in the words of John Greenleaf Whittier, 'drift beyond God's love and care'. Whether we feel, like St. Paul, 'chief of sinners'; struggle to cope with overwhelming guilt, appropriate or inappropriate; or shed inner tears over the failure of our life and service, the knowledge that Christ in his love has penetrated the very depths of human misery and pain is somehow made clear in that descent. From the very gates of hell, there is a road through him that leads towards heaven.

George Macleod, in typically powerful words, makes clear the context in which the good news should be proclaimed. 'The cross should be raised at the centre of the marketplace,' he said, 'Jesus was not crucified in a cathedral between two candles, but on a cross between two thieves, on the town's garbage heap; at a crossroad so cosmopolitan they had to write his title in Hebrew, Latin and Greek; at the kind of place where the cynics talk smut and thieves curse and soldiers gamble . . . That is where he dies. That is what he died for.'

The gospel will be proclaimed in peaceful pulpits and comfortable churches this holy season. And rightly so. But the message of Holy Week cannot be confined to officially spiritual places. It belongs to the marketplace, the High Street, the workshop, the battlefield. For it is at the point where the stark realities of the world meet with the awful reality of Calvary's tree, that the gospel of grace, love and reconciliation is most present.

Jesus's descent into hell is followed by resurrection day. Death is swallowed up in victory. The Easter prayer must be that the Balkan darkness will somehow be followed by an ascent from hell to lasting peace.

A Meditation on the Death of Diana, Princess of Wales: Death Hurts

'Death hurts', I wrote in a Meditation last year⋆. 'Death brings a deep sense of loss, whether it comes as a release from long suffering, as the climax of a fruitful life, in war, by murder, as sudden accident.' A sudden and, in that case, dreadful road crash had brought universal hurt that week.

'In the midst of life we are in death', reads a burial service in *The Book of Common Prayer*. From a religious perspective, as the empty cross proclaims, 'in the midst of death we are in life'. But how difficult to grasp that truth when we are faced by a road crash such as that which has killed the Princess of Wales; by the deaths of two children, murdered while out playing; by the suffering of loved ones struck down by cancer, AIDS, motor neurone disease or Alzheimer's disease.

The questions that flow from such circumstances are not easily met by some philosophical theory or theological dogma. 'Where is God in the circumstances that took the life of the Princess?' 'How can a compassionate God allow two children to fall victim to such an awful combination of circumstances?' If God has given human beings the freedom to do wrong, make mistakes and hurt others, can that same God intervene to overrule the results of our freedom? But surely divine intervention must be possible for an omnipotent God? There are those who have seen miracles who would testify that this is so. But why in some cases and not in others? Why are some healed physically and others are not?

God does not will such suffering. Of the children, Jesus said clearly and with great feeling, 'It is **not** the will of your Father that one of these little ones should perish'. We each have to find our own answers to these impossible questions.

While deep in tragedy is not, however, the time to do it. Bereavement needs prayer rather than propositions, silence rather than words, presence rather than action, touch rather than texts.

Those who cannot take a religious view will find their solace, certainly in the case of the Princess of Wales, in the healing influence of someone never to be forgotten, someone with whose own pain they could empathize, and by whose sensitive compassion they have been blessed. Those of faiths other than Christian will find their strength in the spirituality they know and the beliefs they trust. As one Muslim leader said of the divine compassion: 'He will caress their souls'. Christians, believing in the Incarnation, find there the assurance that, in Jesus, God shared in human pain, pain that reached its climax in awful suffering on a cross. It may just be possible to believe – but only on a long-term view – that 'all things work together for good', through sensing the blessings that can come from human tragedies.

In the midst of someone's death, which hurts us, may we glimpse light and life [34].

---

* 1996 Number 45 in the author's second volume of Meditations entitled *Solitude, Stillness, Serenity.*

34. This Meditation was published on the Saturday after Princess Diana died, on the day of her funeral. By chance, it was placed as the only other item on the full-page obituary to Mother Teresa, who had died the night before (5th September, 1997).

Notes

1. Described in *The Road Taken*, autobiographical reflections by Denis Duncan, 1997. Available from Ecclesia Services, One Cranbourne Road, London N10 2BT (ISBN 0 9529 160 1 0, 1997) Also available from the same source is an audio cassette entitled Be Still and Know, containing 50 Meditations from the book of the same title, personally read by the author.
2. *The Mystery of the Cross*, by Basil Hume, Darton Longman & Todd, 1998.
3. *Creative Silence*, by Denis Duncan, 1980. Available from Ecclesia Services, One Cranbourne Road, London N10 2BT.
4. *Sharing a Grief*, by Sylvia Read, Published by Eccclesia Services, One Cranbourne Road, London N10 2BT (ISBN 0 9529 160 0 2)
5. Article 'Ecstasy' by E. J. Tinsley, in *A Dictionary of Christian Theology*, edited by Alan Richardson, SCM, 1969.
6. Portia in *The Merchant of Venice*, Act III, scene iv.
7. *Gordon Brown, The Biography*, by Paul Routledge, Simon and Shuster, 1998.
8. *In the Heart of the World*, by Mother Teresa, New World Library, 1997.
9. From 'Back to Basics' by Michael Green, quoted in *Ethos, The Ethics in Business Magazine*, August–September 1997.
10. *The Voluntary Society*, by Duane Elgin.
11. *Models of God*, by Sally McFague, SCM Press, 1987.
12. July 1999.
13. Thomas Oden quoted in *The Risks of Freedom*, published by The Pastoral Care Foundation in the Philippines, 1993.
14. *Taste and See: Adventuring into Prayer*, by Margaret Silf, Darton, Longman & Todd.
15. IMAC Cinema, Waterloo, London.
16. *The Fire in These Ashes*, by Joan Chittester, Gracewing, 1997.
17. *Dark Victory*, by Dr Martin Israel, Mowbray, 1995.
18. *Doubt, the Way of Growth*, by Dr Martin Israel, Mowbray, 1997.
19. Performed by Theatre Roundabout, 859 Finchley Road, London NW11 8LX.
20. 1997.
21. Quoted by Donald Nicholl in *Holiness*, Darton, Longman & Todd, 1996
22. Philippians 2:5 (William Barclay's translation).
23. The bomb planted in Omagh in August 1998.
24. *Asking God*, by Oliver Tomkins, Darton, Longman & Todd.
25. The reference is to the England football manager, Glenn Hoddle, who lost his position as a result of a remark that related disability to punishment.
26. A reference to President Clinton's personal problems, 1998.
27. The North London Hospice, 47 Woodside Avenue, London N12 8TF.
28. August 1998.
29. *Godless Morality*, by Richard Holloway, Canongate Books, Edinburgh, 1999.
30. Published just after the death of Diana, Princess of Wales, in August 1997.
31. *Health and Healing, Studies in New Testament Principles and Practice*, by John Wilkinson, Handsel Press, 1980.
32. 1999.
33. *Catching the Dream, New Start for the Millennium*, a Lenten study published by ACTS, Scottish Churches House, Dunblane, Scotland FK15 OAJ, 1999.
34. This Meditation was published on the Saturday after Princess Diana died, on the day of her funeral. By chance, it was placed as the only other item on the full-page obituary to Mother Teresa, who had died the night before (5th September, 1997).